This book is presented to give a public expression of the interpretation of S. H. Froehlich on the Epistles of John. It is commended to your careful consideration by means of the references given and by the entire Word of God.

—Translator

MEDITATIONS

on

THE EPISTLES OF JOHN

Meditations of

S. H. FROEHLICH

Delivered in Zuerich in the Years

1840-1842

(Translated from the German)

06694

VOLUME TWO

APOSTOLIC CHRISTIAN PUBLISHING COMPANY

1327 West Colvin Street

Syracuse, New York

1960

FOREWORD

That the writings of Samuel H. Froehlich (1803-57), which the Lord has preserved to this day, might, *if only in a measure*, accomplish what the spoken word accomplished more than a century ago, was and is a cherished hope of those who have assisted and now assist in the promotion of their circulation.

The writings were not written to no purpose, but no doubt for and against the time which in the foreknowledge, the grace, the patience and longsuffering of God might come after the voice of this shepherd had died away; and certainly there is no greater need for them than now.

One hears though, which is true, "We have the Bible." Yet one hears also, "So then faith cometh by hearing," and "...how shall they hear without a preacher?" Also,
"Not forsaking the assembling of ourselves
together, ... but exhorting one another:"
and these writings are notes which S. H. Froehlich made of his sermons after they were preached.

It was never intended by the writer (or by any who circulate the work) that these writings should replace the Word of God but that they should help to introduce it.

This volume contains all of the writer's notes on the third chapter of the First Epistle of John.

INDEX

Chapter XLVIII

The Right Baptism

November 29, 1840 (Sunday); Morning Meeting
I John 3 : 1 f.

"Behold, what manner of love the Father hath bestowed upon us, that we should be called the sons of God: therefore the world knoweth us not, because it knew him not.

"Beloved, now are we the sons of God, and it doth not yet appear what we shall be: but we know that, when he shall appear, we shall be like him; for we shall see him as he is."

By nature no one is of God, for all are sinners, who come short of the glory of God and bear in them the poison of Adam's sin and the likeness of the devil; and he who is not redeemed therefrom, in this time of grace, by faith in the Gospel of Christ dies eternally on that account (Mark 9; John 8) and he who does not believe it makes God a liar. All, by nature, are in the power of the devil and the Son of God has come in the flesh to release us from him.

These words seem hard and wrong to men, but because they are themselves *hard* in unbelief, the Word of God, accordingly, is like a fire which consumes everything that is of an ungodly nature and like a hammer which breaks rocks: in the believer this takes place here; in the unbeliever, in eternity. In the former it accomplishes salvation and blessedness but in the latter, condemnation (for every sacrifice is salted with fire) and yonder it becomes a worm that does not die and a fire that does not quench.

In order that the spiritual death in Adam may not become eternal death, through Christ's death on the cross it must be given an antidote and outlet; and for this the believers are baptized into the death of Christ and baptism then becomes the transition of the death of Christ upon us and, consequently, also of life, which however is not the case in the baptism of unknowing infants, for their baptism is neither the baptism of John (for the forgiveness of sin) nor the baptism of Christ (for the inner purification from sin), but it is nothing at all, for men in their subsequent life are still dead in sin and the foreskin of the flesh.

For the right baptism of Christ is herein differentiated from the baptism of John: in that it is not merely a baptism of *water* (as is infant baptism), but by virtue of the preceding faith of the Word, it, through the wondrous, hidden working of God, is a real *planting together* with Christ in the likeness of His death (in relation to sin) and of His life (in relation to righteousness), that, instead of the devil, the Son of God takes up a dwelling place in us (John 1:14; Ephesians 5).

> "And the Word was made flesh, and dwelt among us, (and we beheld his glory, the glory as of the only begotten of the Father,) full of grace and truth."

The indwelling sin-poison, as a disease, must receive drainage by baptism in Christ, in a similar way that the morbid matter of smallpox receives it by vaccination. But if vaccination would not immunize one before the outbreak of the disease, it would be useless and would not answer the purpose; and so is infant baptism also useless because it does not answer the purpose and the divine intention of baptism, but rather permits men to remain in sin and deception throughout life. It neither closes up the source of sin nor opens the source of life.

But in him who *by reason of his faith* is baptized into the death of Christ, sin has been put to death and righteousness has been made alive. For that reason the people have really not been baptized. For the baptism of Christ is a baptism of the Spirit and of fire, for purification from indwelling sin and for restoration of the divine image; for even though natural man has a natural mind, the Word of God says,

> "There is none that understandeth, there is none that seeketh after God."

But of what use is a lantern that has no light?

November 29, 1840 (Sunday); Afternoon Meeting

> "Behold, what manner of love the Father hath bestowed upon us, that we should be called the sons of God:"

This, John ascribes to the love of the Father and every pardoned one admits, that, in regard to himself, no more worthiness or aptitude for love could be found in him than in any other sinner. Wherein then does the difference lie between those who attain to sonship of God and those who do not? Could God's love be partial? Does He love some and not others? No, God so loved the world—the ungodly, evil, sinful, lost world—that He gave His Only Begotten Son for it; and just as there is only one God, so there is only one Mediator between God and us, and God desires that all men should be saved and come to the knowledge of the truth.

But when He begins to disclose mens' corruption to

them, their evil first principles, so that they might be healed, they will not permit Him to do it. They do not wish to be "nothing" in their own eyes and consequently have no need for Christ as a Physician and Savior. But those who let themselves be undone, become something to the praise of the grace of God in Christ, for out of Christ they are all as *nothing* before God. It is ever and eternally only Christ the Son of God, the Seed of Abraham and Heir of All Things, and no one else. Thus if one shall really be a child and an heir of God, he must be found in Christ as a new creature, created after the image of God in righteousness and true holiness, where there is no longer Jew and Gentile, etc., but all and in all Christ, and they all one in Him—One new man—as many as there are of them; and because they are in Him, they are also (as He Himself is) the seed of Abraham and, according to the promise, heirs.

But we cannot be otherwise in Him, than that He be also in us as the eternal life, or we might be more faithful than He is and might outdo Him in something. But Christ's life in us is the sure mark and seal that we are *in Him*. Many could say and maintain, "We believe in Christ and have been justified of our sins," without having valid proof of it, namely in His holy, godly life. To be in Christ by faith is the letter of pardon of the children of God but *Christ in us* by His Spirit is the seal on the letter. And if Christ is in us, there is no longer a question what man in and by himself is able or not able to do, but what Christ the Son of God is able to do in regard to a holy walk.

December 1, 1840 (Tuesday); Evening Meeting
I John 3 : 1

The apostle requires that the believers shall see and diligently consider the great love which the Father has bestowed upon them in that they are called the sons of God. The question is how and where can one see this love of God and by what is it recognized. It is revealed only by its working if it has been shed abroad in our hearts, for natural man has no mind for God and His love, not even for that which God does for everyone without exception in this earthly life. Men are so dull, so apathetic and ungrateful that they think that all that takes place is entirely natural, without the incidence of God and His love that they should *acknowledge* and *thank* Him; hence they recognize His love revealed in Christ even less and can see nothing particularly unusual in it because they do not feel their misery in sin and their removal and estrangement from God.

But the children of God, who have tasted the love and kindness of God, cannot be astonished enough that they should be called the sons of God and, compared with this love of the Father, nothing else any longer seems great to them. If an earthly king or a great man on earth would adopt a lost and forsaken beggar-child as his own and his heir (or would provide for a great number of such poor children), we *would* be astonished and would consider such a child (or children) very fortunate and to be envied. But the great of this world despise the lowly among them and consider them unworthy of their notice, although the distance between them is not a shade of the distance of sinful men before God, and had God been inclined toward us as men are toward one another, He would never have regarded us.

But God now commends and proves His love to us in that He gave His Son for us while we were yet sinners—ungodly—and His enemies. Now if we know and consider from what depths of misery God redeems us and to what heights of grace and glory He transfers us, through Christ, we must *reasonably* be astonished, and we can never understand and treasure this love of God enough, or we would consider insignificant all that we have to suffer and deny ourselves of in this world.

And even if it appears as if none envy us of our great blessedness in being children of God, since by reason of it we are despised, mocked, reviled and persecuted, yet it is in just this way that the devil expresses his envy. And if men, whom he uses as tools, do not know what they are doing, he who envies us on account of our salvation, certainly knows it, as he already envied the first two persons because of it and through envy even brought Christ to the cross. So the devil lies in wait for all children of God, that he may rob them again of their treasure and of the crown, be it by affliction or by the lust of the world, and whoever does not know what he has and what is eternally prepared and presented to him by God (I Corinthians 2), is in danger of being deceived by the devil, like Eve. Therefore we must firmly resist the devil by faith so that we save the eternal and veritable and, for it, leave the temporal and perishable behind, as Joseph left his coat in the hand of the adulteress.

Chapter XLIX

The Proof of the Love of God

December 3, 1840 (Thursday); Evening Meeting
I John 3:1 f.

Because no one by nature knows either the Son or the Father (Matthew 11:27; John 8:19), no one by nature is a child of God.

> "All things are delivered unto me of my Father: and no man knoweth the Son, but the Father; neither knoweth any man the Father, save the Son, and he to whomsoever the Son will reveal him."

> "Then said they unto him, Where is thy Father? Jesus answered, Ye neither know me, nor my Father: if ye had known me, ye should have known my Father also."

And because no one can see or has seen the Father, except only in the Son (John 14:7 ff.) (below), an especial revelation of God for the purpose must occur in us, that His nature may be imparted to us by the love of God, poured out into our hearts by the Holy Ghost (Romans 5),

> "If ye had known me, ye should have known my Father also: and from henceforth ye know him, and have seen him.
> "Philip saith unto him, Lord, shew us the Father, and it sufficeth us.
> "Jesus saith unto him, Have I been so long time with you, and yet hast thou not known

me, Philip? he that hath seen me hath seen
the Father; and how sayest thou then, Shew
us the Father?"

which causes such a great change in us that those who
formerly were darkness, originating from the devil, are
now a *light,* originating from God in the Savior. By this
wondrous change and renewal of mind, we can indeed
know who the children of God in the world are, because
the whole world (that is the great masses of men) does
not know God but lies in wickedness, so that all natural
men do the will of their father the devil and not the will
of God because God is not their Father, and their entire
life is a reflection not of the likeness of God but of that
of the devil (Ephesians 2; John 8).

The ultimate reason for the appearance of the Son in
the world was to reveal the Father to us, in that He, by
conversion from darkness and by purification and redemption from sin and unrighteousness, raises us up again
to the estate of sons of God, and by the profound astonishment at the great love of the Father which He reveals
to some who become children of God, it is shown clearly
enough that, by far, not all men enjoy this advantage,
neither have they received this power; otherwise John
would not contrast the whole world with the children of
God: "Therefore [because we have become children of
God] the world knoweth us not, because it knew him not."

For when the apostle says: "Behold, what manner of
love the Father hath bestowed upon us, that we should be
called [are named] the sons of God," he does not at all
mean merely an assumed name, one outside of the truth.
Therefore if the Father calls us His sons, the fact itself
already lies in the name, because then we have been born
of Him and have become participants of His "light"

nature and, as sons of God, are enabled to walk in all righteousness, gentleness and truth.

Otherwise, of course, it is customary that all want to be called children of God and God is made a "Father of All," notwithstanding that the great masses originate from the devil. For if we are children of God by nature already and according to the mind of the flesh, the Son of God has come in vain to destroy the works of the devil in men, and if all *of themselves* are already of God, conversion to Him and a new birth would not be necessary first to become children of God. According to that, the entire Gospel, which declares that men by nature are children of the devil, would be a lie. Because of that, those especially who preach the true Gospel in the world are reviled, rejected and persecuted as teachers of new doctrines— liars, seducers, heretics and sectarians, for they betray and unmask the devil and reveal his works, with which they are well acquainted by their own experience, and he who does not wish to so betray the devil, on account of fear, is really not of God as a child—he, that person, does not know the Father and does not love the Son as his Lord and Redeemer; for the devil and all his children take an assumed, imitated name as do all those who intend to lie and deceive, so as not to be apprehended.

The devil is in the world and reigns in it, but who seeks and finds him there? He is in the hearts of men and yet they consider themselves children of God, and that is not only the worst deception but also the most abominable blasphemy—that the children of the devil consider themselves children of God and dare to pass for them, in all boldness. Now, if one does not know the devil by his works, one will not see him anywhere in the world, even though he is everywhere. The children of God, therefore, must also be recognized by *their* mind and walk in the imitation of Christ, and many who consider themselves believers fall short in this. The true glory of the sonship of God is something entirely different from a pretended, contrived name, but the devil and the world become frightfully angry when we betray him and reveal their deception, and do not recognize carnal men as children of God but give them their real name.

December 6, 1840 (Sunday) ; Morning Meeting
I John 3 : 1 f.

When we hear how profoundly and greatly astonished was the favorite disciple of the Lord at the love of God that some men are called sons of God, how then ought we to feel? This infinite love of God toward men is the least of all things that touches carnal men, at which their hearts of stone should break. They are much more astonished at completely different things that are called great and wonderful in the world. Carnal men judge all things wrongly and perversely, according to the *outward appearance*, not according to their *inner worth*. Only in the light of the Gospel and the love of God in Christ do we know all things in their right worthfulness or worthlessness as God knows them. Then we see that all men are correspondingly high and low by nature, have the same value before God, namely, that of being sinners, who fall short of the glory of God. They are not children of God and cannot be saved, except in Christ only. For these—His enemies—the Father sacrificed His own Son. We see by this proof of the love of God that man in himself has no merit before God, but we also see that he has a very great worth in His sight else Christ would not have died for us.

We must compare and value all men according to the

measuring scale of God. Then all honor and glory of the flesh falls away and no boasting remains unless we, in Christ, become children and heirs of God and joint-heirs with Christ, through a new creation. Sinners, in themselves, are really worth nothing: God has only taken pity on them and drawn His lost property to Himself again. As many as let themselves be reconciled through Christ with God and accept His love are saved and become children of God. But those who despise and spurn this love of God become devils and are wilfully and willingly lost on their own account (Acts 13). Here all human means and help and the inventiveness of education are of no avail toward the healing of the hurt in Adam (which one even with them cannot conceal). These artists become nothing more than hypocrites, and are worse than all other sinners because they wrongly close up the wound with a plaster and then consider themselves better than gross evil doers, whereas before God there is no difference between them.

How much better it is for man to learn to know himself in his gross nakedness and barrenness, to enable him to take off the old man and put on the new one and as a consequence be lifted up to the real dignity of children of God in Christ. Natural man, in his own name, has no access to the Father; before God it must all take place and be done in the name of Jesus. That all men were children of God is so entirely wrong that, rather, of himself, not a single one is that, for God is not the Father of sinners—the devil is—and therefore the children of God, who are in Christ, are no longer sinners either, but the righteous and saints.

December 6, 1840 (Sunday); Afternoon Meeting

Although few on earth are children of God, yet almost no one doubts being one; at least not one of those who are not doubts it, and therefore most men are deceived about their actual standing with God because the devil blinds them. Now, since no one by nature has the right or claim to sonship of God, who then are these that receive this power? They are those who receive Christ the Son (John 1:12 f.).

> "But as many as received him, to them gave he power to become the sons of God, even to them that believe on his name:
> "Which were born, not of blood, nor of the will of the flesh, nor of the will of man, but of God."

But this acceptance takes place by faith in the preached Word, which then is affirmed and sealed by the Spirit of Christ as a power of life unto eternal life. Like the Son, none of the children of God are begotten and born of flesh and blood but of God. It was for this very reason that the Son of God became a Son of man, that He might make the children of Adam (lost sinners), children of God in Himself and give them this fulness of power *in His name.* He has taken on and upon Himself that which was ours, so as to redeem us from sin and out of Satan's power and to give us, instead, that which is His—His glory—which we lack.

Thus the real children of God are indeed to be recognized and even counted in this world of darkness for they are light, begotten of light, so that they, in the name of Jesus, may be a light in this dark world. As many as are sons of God have been called, singled out, and elected thereto of God for His own, and are then also singled out and rejected by the world and their name is put down and rejected as an evil, injurious one, that all might shun them like a communicable contagion among men, because the world considers its own wrong, its evil way the right one, and the one true way to God and eternal life, Christ, the wrong one.

There are indeed some, too, who begin to doubt their sonship of God by natural birth when they believe the Word of Truth and without this struggle of doubt and unbelief, no one comes to the true faith and life of the Son of God or to the full power to become a child of God. But this period of doubting is transitory and forms the passageway from darkness to light, from Satan's power to God. Thus the children of God are well known and recognized: "The Lord knoweth them that are his. And, Let every one that nameth the name of Christ depart from iniquity."

Even the devil and the world know these who no longer are of them but of God, for the light punishes and condemns the darkness and its evil works by its mere presence. The darkness cannot suffer that. It defends itself against the reproving testimony of the light and hates and condemns it in return. But if we, as children of God and of light, are persecuted and reviled by the world, we should rejoice exceedingly and exult triumphantly. What we must suffer with Christ for the sake of truth and righteousness will be richly rewarded to us with eternal rest in heaven. Unbelievers have afflictions in the world too, which they cause themselves by their unrighteousness, in that none will suffer for another, but there follows no rest for them hereafter but eternal unrest.

The way to life, which few find, is a rough one for the flesh only. If the world still recognizes us as its own, we are not of God and if we are children of God in Christ, the friendship of the world has come to an end, because the world does not know Him. We know that we are of God and that the whole world lies in wickedness. Now what still remains if the whole world is on one side? There would of course be few on the other.

Chapter L

"For Without Me Ye Can Do Nothing"

December 8, 1840 (Shrove Tuesday) ; Evening Meeting
I John 3 : 1 f.

"Behold, what manner of love the Father hath bestowed upon us, that we should be called the sons of God: therefore the world knoweth us not, because it knew him not.

"Beloved, now are we the sons of God, and it doth not yet appear what we shall be: but we know that, when he shall appear, we shall be like him; for we shall see him as he is."

The mystery of the sonship of God and the glory of the same is so great that it demands our persevering diligence and zeal, with reflection and prayer, to learn to know and understand in its length and breadth, depth and height, what it means to be a child of God and even then we will know it only in weak outlines. Because of this, it is necessary that we learn to know the Father and the Son rightly, which the world (i.e. all natural men) certainly is unable to do because it is not of God. And as we have been of the world also, we cannot otherwise know God or be His children unless we, at a time in our life by the call and election of God, have *become* His children, and the more our glimpse into this mystery is expanded, the more we must be astonished at it and in enchantment be carried away from all that is earthly, visible and temporal, be it sorrow or joy, advantage or self-denial in this world, in order that in the Spirit we may be at home with the Lord, immovable and undistracted (I Corinthians 7: 35).

"And this I speak for your own profit; not that I may cast a snare upon you, but for that which is comely, and that ye may attend upon the Lord without distraction."

Our presence in the present evil world, as it is, carries along with it so many disturbances and distractions that we need not seek or give ourselves over to them, but on the contrary should rather watch and pray and battle against them so as to make our calling and election sure and to perfect our holiness in the fear of God. If we consider how great beyond all measure is the promise that the living God will dwell in us and walk about on earth, we *reasonably* ought to ask, "Where is the Lord God of Elijah?" (II Kings 2) for if we are indifferent—indolent, absent-minded—in the world in the thoughts and meditations of our heart, we slight taking care of the treasure which we carry in earthen vessels and are in danger of losing, and in that case experience nothing of the overwhelming greatness of the power of God that worked so wondrously in the believers and saints of the early times because they *abode continuously in Him, prayed without ceasing,* and consequently took from His fulness, grace for grace.

For those believers, of themselves, were no stronger than we are. A Paul could and would boast of nothing of himself except his weakness, but such powers as worked in them came from their abiding in Him and drawing from Him and, by reason thereof, His abiding in them. "For without me ye can do nothing" was the instruction

(John 15). They had not the source of power *in themselves,* neither had they a supply from which they could have subsisted and worked independently of Him for a time, but their power lay in their faith and love to the Lord, Who will reveal Himself to His own in just this, that He gives them what they have need of and succors them as often as they entreat Him. Then we experience the nearness of the living God Whom the world does not know; then faith becomes an active profession.

Why are men at present—yes, even the believers— so weak and unfruitful in good works, so despairing in affliction? Not because the power of the Lord could have diminished but because men are so competely distracted by earthly things, devoid of faith and love to the Lord; otherwise the same power would manifest itself in them as in those past times. But men, on account of their spiritual indolence and lukewarmness, no longer know and experience the living God and yet it would be so necessary to apply this short time of grace entirely toward this cardinal and central point, around which the entire life of the children of God revolves, namely to work out their salvation with fear and trembling. Certainly this was the unremitting prayer and supplication of the Apostle Paul for all believers, that God might give them 'enlightened eyes of understanding to know what the hope of His calling really is, the riches of the glory of His inheritance in the saints and the exceeding greatness of His power in the believers (Ephesians 1).'

Pastor Lucius once said that if a man would always live in God, he would always be prepared to preach, which utterance was set down to his pride and foolishness.

December 10, 1840 (Thursday); Evening Meeting
I John 3:1 f.

In order to get a clear glimpse into the mystery of godliness and our sonship of God ['*God is manifested in the flesh*' (above all in the person of Jesus of Nazareth, but also in all who accept Christ the Son and *by His Holy Spirit receive and have Jesus Himself dwelling in them substantially so that they too may become sons of God in Him*)], we must learn to know the one, true, living God, Whom the world does not know, for eternal life lies therein. But the right knowledge of God consists herein, that He is a Spirit (John 4), Whom man cannot serve with formal profession and rituals after the manner of the law, but Whom we must worship in *spirit* and in *truth*.

Children of God enter into this new relationship to the Father *in Christ*. By communication of *His own Spirit* (as the personal Plenipotentiary of the Son with us), they become participants of His divine nature; foster an uninterrupted association in the Spirit with Him (i.e., pray without ceasing) and therefore are never left alone in this world; can make known to Him all that is of concern to them; are heard by Him and receive their petitions from Him, that they may do nothing except as before His countenance, for His glory, to be acceptable to Him. These are the children of God who thus kindredly know the living God and have Him in their very hearts; for the mystery of godliness always subsists herein, that *God is manifest in the flesh* through Christ and His Spirit of power and love and sanctification. By that, the children of God at all times are blessed and strong although they of themselves are incapable, weak, miserable (II Corinthians 3).

But if anyone enjoying such fellowship and relationship with God, in whose heart Christ works and dwells and walks about in the world, would confess before other men that Christ is in him, not only would he be mocked like a fool and a fanatic about it, but actually the devil and the world cannot tolerate Christ's Spirit in us, so that we might live and walk according to Christ's mind and to all the good pleasure of God, without inquiring about the honor of men, for the beginning of wisdom is the fear of God and its perfection the love of God, which does all His will. But if Christ thus dwells in us, the world, in which the spirit of the devil reigns and whose children are therefore his and not God's, hates and persecutes us. But the living God in us is still mightier than the devil is in the world and if we are constantly in God and God is in us, a secret fear is made to creep over our enemies.

December 15, 1840 (Tuesday); Evening Meeting
I John 3:1

Since it is now in itself clear that *not all* but only *some* men are children of God (because the world does not know God), it is also evident that God dwells and works in His children in an altogether peculiar way and that He keeps them under His immediate guardianship and rearing and in the discipline of the Spirit, about which no one knows anything except the one who experiences it. For, since the world lies in wickedness, is disobedient to the voice of God and contradicts it and will pursue its own way, God lets it go its way and exercises no such direct judgment in the hearts of unbelievers as He exercises in His own children (so that they may not sin and so be not condemned with the world, I Corinthians 11). By this very extraordinary, inherent Spirit-discipline, one recognizes the children of God, and he who does not experience this inner judgment of all the thoughts and desires of his heart, does not know the living God (Who as a Spirit knows and penetrates all things) and is therefore no child of God, because it is not enough to know and to appreciate (according to one's own concept) that God knows and searches all things and in spite of it to live as ungodly as if He did not know or inquire about what we think and say and do.

Chapter LI

The Bearers of the Cross

If we truly know God, all our thoughts and desires must necessarily be directed upon Him, for He alone is deserving and worthy that we continually occupy ourselves with Him and consider all else in this His light, that we may not be removed from the simplicity in Christ, which in this world is so easily possible and so quickly done if we do not constantly watch over our hearts and what goes on in them.

But where God fills, reigns in, and judges the heart with His light so that all that is in it is illumined, there it is impossible for evil, idle, pointless conversation, nonsensical behavior, etc., to come forth, which is unbecoming of children of God and saints, but rather *that* is possible which *is* becoming and which serves for needful edification (Matthew 15; Ephesians 4 and 5; I Peter 1), since the mouth speaks only that with which the heart overflows, and if evil were not in it in an overflowing measure, it would not come forth from it. And where that happens, there one does not have God but a dead idol. It is true, that the children of God can also become vapid and unsavory when they forget themselves and God, but otherwise they should always have salt with them and season all they do and say with it. But if they are disobedient to the inner discipline and righteousness of the Spirit and transgress in word or deed, they fall under the judgment of the church which the saints must execute among themselves (not over the world which God will judge).

There are no other children of God than the saints, and since there are few saints in the world, who at all times do what pleases the Father (like the Son), there are few children of God, who *for that reason* are hated and despised so much by the many who insist upon being right in their wayward carnal mind, so that the converted ones naturally must be wrong and untoward in the eyes of the world.

December 17, 1840 (Thursday) ; Evening Meeting
I John 3 : 1 f.

Concerning the state of relationship to God, John makes the distinction between the present and the future. There indeed are some on earth who can in truth say, "We are now the children of God," because they know and perceive it by the new divine nature and disposition of the Spirit they have received from the Father and, thus far, are not unrevealed but made manifest (even to the world, which nevertheless does not recognize them because of it, except as fools, seducers and the seduced who have fallen away from the faith of the church), for the children of God are spiritual, no longer carnal. But what they shall be in the future revelation of their glory with Christ is *now* still unrevealed even to them, for they walk by faith and not by sight, and thus the life of faith in the Son of God is an intermediate state between the *darkness* of the present world and the revealed beholding of the future one.

The children of God are, and walk, in the light and not in darkness, but their existence in the future world is still puzzling to them (I Corinthians 13). All that they know about it is that they will be like Christ because He, for that reason, has gone on before them to prepare a place for His own and then is to come again and take them to Himself so that they may be forever where He is (John 14). No eye has yet seen and no ear heard what the future glory of the children of God is, but to those whom it concerns, God reveals it by His Spirit, that they run not in uncertainty like the masses, who want to be saved by the power and goodness of the Father because they do not know that it depends, not upon man's own willing and running, but upon the mercy of God *in Christ* to be renewed in Him to the divine nature.

And that is not the case with anyone who does not know in what the future glory subsists, so that everyone who has himself not experienced this change from darkness to light is deceived by his hope of eternal life: for, as Christ is the Life, so is He the only Way to the Father also and we must go forth and be perfected upon the same way to glory, upon which He Himself has gone before us, namely, through the sufferings of this time; for as soon as Christ is in us and we are in Him, the world fails to recognize us any longer and persecutes us for His sake. It is always Christ Who has to suffer and what we suffer for Him for the sake of righteousness and truth (without cause), is the real cross that we shall bear for Him in order to be His disciples and followers. For just as the name of Christ is misused in the world, so is each and every kind of suffering of man unrightly called a cross. Surely they do not suffer for Christ's sake but on their own account; not for the sake of righteousness, but on account of sin.

In the world the cross of Christ is the greatest reproach, but before God it is the greatest honor (so entirely different is the mind of the world from the mind of God); and as suffering for Christ depends upon His life being in us, so, again, does the future glory depend upon the suffering being for Christ's sake. Just as one is *ashamed of Christ* who will not share His suffering with Him in this world, so another will *deny Christ* before men who does not have His life in him and proves it by his entire walk.

Under these circumstances, in the future world we shall be greatly surprised at the revelation of the children of God when we see the (supposed) children of the kingdom cast out (those who for a certainty had counted upon the inheritance) and on the other hand only the despised and rejected cross-bearers of this world sit at the table with Abraham, Isaac, and Jacob in the kingdom of God (those who had not at all been regarded as the right believers but as fools and irrational people); for Christ divides the kingdom among us as the Father has allotted it to Him, i.e., if we have endured with Him in His temptations in this world (Luke 22:28 ff.; Matthew 8:11 f.),

"Ye are they which have continued with me in my temptations.

"And I appoint unto you a kingdom, as my Father hath appointed unto me;

"That ye may eat and drink at my table in my kingdom, and sit on thrones judging the twelve tribes of Israel."

"And I say unto you, That many shall come from the east and west, and shall sit down with Abraham, and Isaac, and Jacob, in the kingdom of heaven.

"But the children of the kingdom shall be cast out into outer darkness: there shall be weeping and gnashing of teeth."

for cowards, with all their appearance of godliness, are not any better before God than the revealed adulterers and liars (Revelation 2: 8 f.).

"And unto the angel of the church in Smyrna write; These things saith the first and the last, which was dead, and is alive;

"I know thy works, and tribulation, and poverty, (but thou art rich) and I know the blasphemy of them which say they are Jews, and are not, but are the synagogue of Satan."

Chapter LII

Union With God

December 20, 1840 (Sunday); Morning Meeting
I John 3: 1 ff.

"Behold, what manner of love the Father hath bestowed upon us, that we should be called the sons of God: therefore the world knoweth us not, because it knew him not.

"Beloved, now are we the sons of God, and it doth not yet appear what we shall be: but we know that, when he shall appear, we shall be like him; for we shall see him as he is.

"And every man that hath this hope in him purifieth himself, even as he is pure.

"Whosoever committeth sin transgresseth also the law: for sin is the transgression of the law.

"And ye know that he was manifested to take away our sins; and in him is no sin."

Man's designation is his union with God. This, however, has become impossible in Adam because of sin or the disposition of the flesh, which is enmity toward God. The old man is of no account and cannot be made new and good. No matter how much one mends and patches him up by human artifice, education and culture, he still remains the old man, a villain and a hypocrite. He must die and be put off with Christ on the cross and, in place of him, we must put on Christ, the New Man and Other Adam, and be found in Him as children of God and a new creation, besides which nothing is acceptable in God's sight.

The law and circumcision do not amend the harm in Adam (Philippians 3; II Corinthians 5; Galatians 5 and 6). If the man in Adam were right and could be saved, the Son of God would not have had to come in the flesh and would have died in vain and, accordingly, the entire Gospel would be a lie. But if we, in Adam, have lost our sonship-right in God, we must be and abide in Christ until His manifestation; we must have put Him on in the Spirit and be minded as was He as a Child of God. Then we may no longer look to the first Adam or we shall deny the Second One, Who is mightier and One with the Father. We must learn to know Him well as the Son of God if we shall have a correct knowledge of our sonship of God, not a false and carnal one as have men of the world, who understand nothing at all of the Spirit of God and think God is like the devil if we, as sinners and children of Adam, should be children of God; whereas only the saints and elect are they, who have become a light in the Lord, and may truly boast of Him, not conceitedly and falsely, but because they are in Him and He by His Spirit is in them.

The sonship of God has two degrees however, one of the present time and one in eternity; namely, it is now hidden and in eternity is revealed with Christ in glory. Yet, even now, the children of God, as a light in the world, are not so obscure that men should not see and recognize them: it is only that they are not recognized in the world for what they are, as little as Christ was recognized as the Son of God. The Jews really thought they knew Him and knew whence He was—namely the son of Joseph, was of Nazareth—and took offense at this lowly veil of disguise, His human appearance, and yet did not know Him (John 7:27 ff.; 9:29 f.),

> "Howbeit we know this man whence he is: but when Christ cometh, no man knoweth whence he is.
> "Then cried Jesus in the temple as he taught, saying, Ye both know me, and ye know whence I am: and I am not come of myself, but he that sent me is true, whom ye know not.
> "But I know him: for I am from him, and he hath sent me."

> "We know that God spake unto Moses: as for this fellow, we know not from whence he is.
> "The man answered and said unto them, Why herein is a marvelous thing, that ye know not from whence he is, and yet he hath opened mine eyes."

and so all children of God in this world are also unknown, "and yet well known; as dying, and, behold, we live;"—

"as deceivers, and yet true; (II Corinthians 6)." But whoever, now in this time, does not attain to conformity with Christ in mind and spirit will not attain to it later in eternity.

Thus, it is clear that our earthly body is not the hindrance to a godly life, for not only has Christ appeared in the same flesh and blood that we are in and still did not sin, but we ourselves, as children of God, must glorify the Father with our body also (I Corinthians 6) and work the works of God. One does not enter into the kingdom of God so easily through Christ the Crucified as men imagine, but with the living Christ in our heart, whereby we are united with the Father also, as is the Son; and unless our 'righteousness should infinitely exceed the righteousness of the scribes and Pharisees, we cannot enter into the kingdom of God (Matthew 5).'

December 20, 1840 (Sunday); Afternoon Meeting

Into what kind of relationship to God do we enter when we become His children? In what kind of relation does a child stand with his father? He comes from him (was formerly in him) and receives his nature and his likeness. Through spiritual generation and the birth from God in Christ, we do indeed become not only angels, but something much higher—as much higher as the Son is higher than all angels (Hebrews 1). Only in Christ, the Only Begotten of the Father, do we find the right relationship of sonship of God: He, alone, is the Image of the Father, the Reflection of His Glory and the Expression of His Being. God has created innumerable beings but none stand on the same plane with the Only Begotten Son. However this very One the Father has given for us, and all who are in Christ become like Him and one with Him;

accordingly, higher than all other created beings, higher than Adam was before the fall.

Christ, as the Only Begotten Son, is also the only Heir of the Father and, besides, out of Him, no angel and no human being, not even the children of God, shall individually and independently—each one for himself, as so many sons and heirs of God—share the relationship of the Son to the Father; but all shall jointly do so, as one in the Son (one new man, Ephesians 2), as a community of the saints (the body of Christ), whose Head and Savior He is, and they—among themselves members of the same—have been made to drink of one Spirit, and whoever is then not one of them, does not belong to Christ and cannot be saved because *out of Christ* there is no salvation.

Woe unto us, if we force the Word of God and want to make the way to salvation broader than it is, as so many who abide in sin and deceive themselves about sonship with God, do to their own harm, when there indeed is no sin in Christ; instead He died for it, that He might take away and abolish our sin and destroy the work of the devil. But we cannot *otherwise* be in Christ or put Him on so as to appear in His person before the Father, unless we take off the devil, or the old man, with his works. Both, the old and the new, cannot live jointly in one person. Neither is it required of man himself that he live as Christ lived—without sin, but it is Christ *Himself* Who can do it and does do it in us because it is His nature which He cannot deny.

Those, therefore, who will excuse themselves with their human weakness for sin, are not in Christ; otherwise He would also be in them and He is not weak, but strong and He cannot sin, but can do only righteousness. Of this we are convinced. So there is a lack of the right knowledge of the mystery: "Christ in us, the hope of glory," because men do not know what "to be in Christ" is and means and if we should be unable to find a purified church of sanctified children of God anywhere on earth, it would take nothing at all away from the power and the truth of the Word of God.

All who do not *here* become fitted for being in Christ, because they are not willing to sacrifice their carnal mind, which begets enmity and strife, will yonder not belong to the holy church, which nevertheless will once be revealed with the Son, to Whom the inheritance belongs. Therefore it depends upon this, that we learn to know the living God, how He as a Spirit is present everywhere and knows all things and dispenses all things, etc. Therein lies eternal life. He who so communes with God *has* eternal life; he who does not so know God has not the true God but merely an idol of his imagination, and he cannot pray to overcome the world.

December 22, 1840 (Tuesday); Evening Meeting
I John 3 : 2 ff.

> "Beloved, now are we the sons of God, and it doth not yet appear what we shall be: but we know that, when he shall appear, we shall be like him; for we shall see him as he is.
>
> "And every man that hath this hope in him purifieth himself, even as he is pure.
>
> "Whosoever committeth sin transgresseth also the law: for sin is the transgression of the law.
>
> "And ye know that he was manifested to take away our sins; and in him is no sin."

Manifestation of the *sonship* of God is accomplished in two stages or terms, in such a way that those who shall be made manifest therein in eternity, must have been made so by Christ in the time of grace, for since we by nature, as sinners, have no fellowship with God and no right of approach to Him, because we do not know Him, this right must be bestowed upon us by the Son, Who, for this very purpose, entered as our Mediator, between God and men, that by Him we might be purified from sin and enmity and darkness. Therefore Christ is our only Way to the Father, to Whom we must go and with Whom we must walk *here,* so as to obtain the necessary purification in this transition to appear afterwards as He is. For if an artist would unveil and exhibit a great work, he must have created it beforehand in retirement; so also, if God would reveal His children as images of His Son and unveil His gems in the future world, we must have been prepared for it in this time.

But purification is brought about in a twofold way: in part by water with reference to the sins formerly committed, for their forgiveness; in part by the Holy Spirit and fire with regard to indwelling sin, as the mother of all committed sins, for her complete undoing, dismissal and destruction, that the purified may thenceforth not defile themselves but perfect their holiness in the fear of God (II Corinthians 7:1).

> "Having therefore these promises, dearly beloved, let us cleanse ourselves from all filthiness of the flesh and spirit, perfecting holiness in the fear of God."

For this reason John the Baptist had to precede Christ to prepare the way with a baptism of repentance for the forgiveness of sins to the contrite, but John directed them to the Greater, One Who should come after him and Who first would *rightly* baptize or purify them with the Holy

Ghost and fire, because the inherited sin of Adam cannot be washed away but must be burned out. While we pass through the world by faith in the Son of God, we must be molten by this fire in the fellowship of life and suffering; we must be made pliant and be shaped into a new form, after the image of the Son. Then we *know* that we are of God and that in the revelation of the Son and of His children we shall be like Him (Christ), because He Himself dwells and walks in us by His Spirit and our fellowship is with the Father and the Son.

If we thus appreciate the glory of the children of God, we can no longer have fellowship with darkness and its unfruitful works (II Corinthians 6; Ephesians 5) but must rather reprove them, for we at all times walk in the light of His holy presence, in the living awareness that we are in Him and that He is in us; and if we always bore that in mind, we would never forget God, never talk or act foolishly, but would always be as the wise. For men sin only for the reason that they do not know God, do not have Him and His fear before their eyes (Romans 3), do not believe that God will bring them to judgment because of their evil speakings and deeds, and punish them. Thus the ungodly one (he who forgets God) is the mother of all sin and unrighteousness. Children of God must be enlightened to the extent that they, so to speak, learn to see with the eyes of God.

December 25, 1840 (Christmas); Morning Meeting
I John 3:3 ff.

As we have become children of the devil through Adam, so through Christ we must anew become children of God: it depends entirely upon whether we live in the spirit or in the flesh. Those who live according to the flesh and want to be free are taken captive, bound and darkened in the spirit by Satan, but in those who live in the spirit and *are* free, the flesh is bound and forced to obedience by the spirit to do the will of God, as well as to suffer in this life for Christ's sake.

This is the struggle which is appointed to us—between flesh and spirit—not *out of us* but right *in* us, that we give the devil no room in his temptations of the flesh, but in the spirit live for God and remain free and become blessed. Carnal men have entirely mistaken conceptions of freedom and well-being, in that they take the risk in just those matters in which they are servants of destruction and wretched in time and eternity. For as long as we serve sin, we are free from righteousness but if we have been *freed* from sin, we have become *servants* of righteousness and as death is the wages of sin, so is eternal life the reward of righteousness (Romans 6), and no one can serve both masters (Matthew 6).

There is no middle way and there are no half-Christians before God, although there are such in this world, who would like to share between Christ and Belial, between God and mammon, but with respect to the inheritance they fare no better with God than those who do not believe at all. Thence it is a question of what one will decide and what one will choose for himself—servitude of the spirit or servitude of the flesh, affliction now and glory thereafter, or good living now and condemnation thereafter—for whoever, through Christ and in Christ, becomes free according to the spirit from the inner power of the devil is on *that* account all the more subjected to the outward violence of Satan according to the flesh, but yet he is free, even though he were cast into prison with Christ, because the spirit cannot be taken captive except by sin only.

December 27, 1840 (Sunday) ; Morning Meeting
I John 3 : 2 ff.

It would be hard for me to leave the word, "Now are we the sons of God," without it having become clear to all of us what it means to *be* a son of God, so that no one should be deceived about it, for if our sonship is a fact, the inheritance follows of itself, even though we now do not yet understand what it will be. As children of God we must be as Jesus was and since we did not see Him in the flesh, we must learn to know Him by the Word and in the Spirit, so as to pattern ourselves after Him, and we shall choose no other man for our model than He Who has come into the world and died on the cross for this, that He might separate us anew from the sin that has come upon us through Adam. For if he who has sinned has not seen or known Jesus, then only he who does not sin knows Him because it is not Christ but the devil who sins. But if Christ is in us, the devil no longer is, and we would not have to serve him.

The apostles (Peter, Paul and others) by nature were not better and stronger than we are, but after they had put on Christ, they became strong in Him and so conformable to Him that they again, as visible images of Christ, could be an example *in the imitation of Him* for others, and if one could be an example then all can be, because it is not *our* strength and endeavor but the grace and gift of God in Christ (Ephesians 2).

Chapter LIII

The Goal and Designation

With the end in view, our goal and designation now is this: that, in this world, we shall be as was the Son of man Jesus, so that we may be His brothers and sisters, who do the will of the Father. In this respect, there are indeed *many* who will be saved as *members* of the body of Christ. Thus Christ is the *Firstborn* among many brethren who become children of God, but with respect to the *inheritance* they are but *one* in Christ, as *one body*, and whoever is not found in this oneness cannot inherit since the inheritance is dependent upon sonship.

Thus there is a double relationship in Christ by His being the Son of man and of God. As the son of man He desires to be multiplied and is the Firstborn among *many*, but as the Son of God He is ever and eternally only One, the Only Begotten of the Father (John 1; Romans 8; Hebrews 2). As the Son of man we must now already know Him for therein we become like Him in His holy life and suffering on earth so as to be children of God; but as the Son of God in His glory, we only afterwards shall learn to know Him.

John sums up the life of Christ in the word "pure." Just as He was holy, innocent, undefiled, set apart from sinners and made higher than the heavens (Hebrews 7:26) (below), so shall we, in Him, also be set apart from sinners and be higher than the angels (I Peter 2 and 3), who are merely servants for our salvation.

> "For such an high priest became us, who is holy, harmless, undefiled, separate from sinners, and made higher than the heavens;"

Children of God are pure and holy, free from sin, and they must be so in Christ, for in Him there is no sin and anyone who abides *in* Him does not sin. Because of that, we dare not be frightened about the impossibility of the thing, but rather about this, that we are not of that circumstance by reason of our own fault, for if we truly desired and longed so to be, it would be granted to us also according to His promise, for God is not a man that He should lie or that He would have to repent of something.

Should we not be—or are not becoming—like Christ, the reason is that we do not receive Him, for even though no one at present seeks God first, of himself, but God seeks us first, as the lost, the ungodly and sinnners, we nevertheless must still seek Him afterwards in return, must knock, must ask that He cleanse us from our former sins with His blood and give us His Holy Spirit Who makes us free from the law of sin and death in our members (Romans 8). Thus God indeed *anticipates* us with His grace and offer, but it is all the more worthy of punishment if we do not respond to Him and pray for and receive His gift, for whoever does not ask for the Holy Spirit does not receive Him because that person is not concerned about Him and yet, nowhere at all is there life, peace and joy for us except in a holy life in Christ.

December 27, 1840 (Sunday); Afternoon Meeting
I John 3:2 ff.

> "Beloved, now are we the sons of God, and it doth not yet appear what we shall be: but we know that, when he shall appear, we shall be like him; for we shall see him as he is.
>
> "And every man that hath this hope in him purifieth himself, even as he is pure.
>
> "Whosoever committeth sin transgresseth

also the law: for sin is the transgression of the law.

"And ye know that he was manifested to take away our sins; and in him is no sin.

"Whosoever abideth in him sinneth not: whosoever sinneth hath not seen him, neither known him."

John ascribes to the children of God the ability to *purify themselves,* or to keep themselves from *new defilement* after their former sins of the time of ignorance (I Timothy 1) have once been forgiven and remitted unto them and they at a time in their life have been cleansed from them by faith in the blood of Christ (John 13; Hebrews 10). For with this great, complete absolution, they also receive the power of the new life to do the good (Ephesians 2) and its preservation is not difficult for him who has received the true grace of God (I Peter 5), and although, by nature, we have no ability for the good because we are dead in sin, we nevertheless receive it in Christ and we should take care that we have not received the grace of God in vain (II Corinthians 6).

For the purpose of Christ's appearance in the flesh is our purification from sin or the killing-off of the same in us, that the life of the righteousness of God follow thereupon and that no further defilement by sin be mingled with it; for the Lord praises those only who have not defiled their garments and promises them that they shall walk with Him "in white, for they are worthy (Revelation 3)." For, even though it can happen that a cleansed and pardoned one in Christ through inadvertence is overtaken by faults (Galatians 6), he could surely have avoided being overtaken, by faithfulness and he will at least free himself from it again as soon as he becomes aware of it, for indifference and carelessness with respect to new defilement draws death upon it.

For it its an entirely different matter with the sins of a pardoned one than with the sins of an unpardoned one who is still dead in sin and the foreskin of the flesh: for the pardoned one has passed over from death unto life and God has put the law of the Spirit of the life in Christ Jesus in his heart and if he should now sin, it must happen either by thoughtlessness in an unguarded moment (not from habit and then it is not a deadly sin), or it happens voluntarily and with seeing eyes against a definite commandment or the forbiddance of God, as did Adam's sin, through which single transgression of the law of God all men have died along with him; and this first death in Adam must be removed anew from us by Christ and we must give back to the devil what we have received from him in Adam so that death (sin) no longer may be in us but life (righteousness).

This happens in the baptism of the believer because it is a baptism into Christ's death, with which a formal renunciation of the devil and his works is connected on the part of the believer. This, however, is not the case in the baptism of unknowing children for sin dwells and reigns in them afterwards despite baptism and, further, sin is not accountable to them up until the law. For the children of Adam do not sin in the same way that Adam himself sinned—knowingly and voluntarily, but natural men sin blindly, by inborn habit and ignorance of God. Only when the law enters does a certain resemblance to the sin of Adam become prevalent, because it is a definite commandment that is transgressed by sin and, through that, natural sin, by the very knowledge of it, becomes condemnable so that man may be converted therefrom and may in the only Mediator—Christ—seek and find forgiveness, redemption and life, according to the Gospel.

Transgression of a *definite,* given *commandment* is the real character of a wilful, voluntary or mortal sin and that, again, in the pardoned man in Christ is then exactly the same situation as it was in the case of Adam *with this difference only,* that the first death extended itself to *all* men (without complicity and accountability, Romans 5:12 ff.) (below) whereas; not to preserve grace or one-self in grace draws the second death upon it only *for each such pardoned one* who transgresses.

"Wherefore, as by one man sin entered into the world, and death by sin; and so death passed upon all men, for that all have sinned:

"(For until the law sin was in the world: but sin is not imputed when there is no law.

"Nevertheless death reigned from Adam to Moses, even over them that had not sinned after the similitude of Adam's transgression, who is the figure of him that was to come.

"But not as the offence, so also is the free gift. For if through the offence of one many be dead, much more the grace of God, and the gift by grace, which is by one man, Jesus Christ, hath abounded unto many.

"And not as it was by one that sinned, so is the gift: for the judgment was by one to condemnation, but the free gift is of many offences unto justification.

"For if by one man's offence death reigned by one; much more they which receive abundance of grace and of the gift of righteousness shall reign in life by one, Jesus Christ.)

"Therefore as by the offence of one judgment came upon all men to condemnation; even so by the righteousness of one the free gift came upon all men unto justification of life.

"For as by one man's disobedience many were made sinners, so by the obedience of one shall many be made righteous.

"Moreover the law entered, that the offence might abound. But where sin abounded, grace did much more abound:

"That as sin hath reigned unto death, even so might grace reign through righteousness unto eternal life by Jesus Christ our Lord."

Therefore, because sin is no longer inherent in a pardoned child of God but is purged out in relation to the former sins by Christ's blood and in relation to new defilement by Christ's Spirit (preservation of the purification), a man of God can, like Adam, sin only through temptation. But a child of God shall arm himself with grace, and fight and be guided by it, against the temptations of the devil, and shall resist every impure impulse already in the bud so that it may not be able to take root. Before such an equipage of armament and a stronghold of God, the devil must flee and he cannot touch him who watches over himself, as we see by the example of Christ the Son of man (Matthew 4).

Now just as sin in man or the first death is the devil himself through his lying spirit of pride, of lust of the flesh, lust of the eyes, etc., so is righteousness or the new life in Christ, God Himself in His children; and each one who has felt the curse of the law and condemnation in his conversion must thenceforth guard himself from sin and new defilement in the manner portrayed in the proverb: *"Die gebrannten Kinder fuerchten das Feuer"* (Burnt children dread the fire). And if through recognition of our lost condition in Adam, we have not become wise in relation to sin and the devil, we then boast in vain of the forgiveness of our former sins in the blood of Christ: we either have never reached after and obtained forgiveness or have not preserved it and have lost it again (II Peter 2). And as the angels who sinned and forsook their origin became devils and darkness, and as Adam *by a single sin* hurled himself and all his children into death, so it happens to those also who do not preserve and use *to the end* the grace of life granted them in Christ so as to live for God in holiness and righteousness.

And there indeed is a rising up from the fall of Adam and the first death possible through Christ because it is unmerited on our part; but there is no rising from voluntary backsliding and the second death again possible. There the avowal of the prodigal son is no longer of any avail; it is the same situation as under the law of Moses: "I have sinned against Heaven and Thee (Hebrews 6 and 10; II Peter 2)." Here again sin is voluntary and for that there is left no other sacrifice.

Therefore both are lost in eternity, those who have not accepted the grace of life in their time and those who have not preserved it to the end so as to be saved. Now just as a pure heart beholds God in the Spirit and has a joyful association with Him under the seal of a good conscience, so an impure, a sinful, dark heart is excluded from fellowship with God and is unfit for His kingdom, and the seal upon it is a bad conscience that must fear eternal death on the day of judgment.

— END OF YEAR 1840 —

> "The name of the Lord is a strong tower:
> the righteous runneth into it, and is safe."
>
> —Proverbs 18:10

Sinners, hypocrites and liars cover their sins and display instead, with great ostentation, their erroneously imputed good works; the children of God, on the other hand, hide their good works and instead reveal their faults and make them known (Matthew 6; Luke 18: 9 ff.).

> "And he spake this parable unto certain which trusted in themselves that they were righteous, and despised others:
> "Two men went up into the temple to pray; the one a Pharisee, and the other a publican.
> "The Pharisee stood and prayed thus with himself, God, I thank thee, that I am not as other men are, extortioners, unjust, adulterers, or even as this publican.
> "I fast twice in the week, I give tithes of all that I possess.
> "And the publican, standing afar off, would not lift up so much as his eyes unto heaven, but smote upon his breast, saying, God be merciful to me a sinner."

One, whose heart does not censure or accuse itself before God, is either a most faithful saint or one of the worst hypocrites (I Corinthians 4:4; I John 3:21).

> "For I know nothing by myself; yet am I not hereby justified: but he that judgeth me is the Lord."

> "Beloved, if our heart condemn us not, then have we confidence toward God."

The spirit of the world is high-minded and yet it strives after that which is here below and from beneath (of the world); the Spirit of God (in His children) is humble and meek and yet it strives after that which is above and from above (I John 4:1 ff.).

"Beloved, believe not every spirit, but try the spirits whether they are of God: because many false prophets are gone out into the world.

"Hereby know ye the Spirit of God: Every spirit that confesseth that Jesus Christ is come in the flesh is of God:

"And every spirit that confesseth not that Jesus Christ is come in the flesh is not of God: and this is that spirit of antichrist, whereof ye have heard that it should come; and even now already is it in the world.

"Ye are of God, little children, and have overcome them: because greater is he that is in you, than he that is in the world.

"They are of the world: therefore speak they of the world, and the world heareth them.

"We are of God: he that knoweth God heareth us; he that is not of God heareth not us. Hereby know we the spirit of truth, and the spirit of error."

Chapter LIV

The New Year of Grace

January 1, 1841 (Friday); Morning Meeting

The children of this world are accustomed to wish one another well and to give gifts at New Year's, but their wishes are empty and their gifts vain. Men themselves cannot fulfil their good wishes; that alone is God's matter. However, if we do not bless one another in our hearts in the name of the Lord, then God also will not bring about fulfilment; but if we wish one another the veritable good—God's kingdom and sonship, then God also will bring it about and then we also must serve and help one another to obtain it, if it shall not be empty wishing. Only God gives us the right kind of New Year's gift and he who receives it has, in truth, come into a *New Year of Grace* (Luke 4:19; II Corinthians 6:1 f.).

"To preach the acceptable year of the Lord."

"We then, as workers together with him, beseech you also that ye receive not the grace of God in vain.

"(For he saith, I have heard thee in a time accepted, and in the day of salvation have I succoured thee: behold, now is the accepted time; behold, now is the day of salvation.)"

For to what greater thing than sonship of God can we attain, inasmuch as we can in truth say, "We are now sons of God," and the best part, the inheritance with Christ, according as we have been faithful here for a time as children of obedience, is still kept in store and hidden for us in heaven (I Peter 1). But just as earthly parents include for their children's New Year's gift a rod as a warning against disobedience and for its punishment, so also the Heavenly Father wraps up a rod with His New Year's gift to rear us in righteousness, so that we may attain to sanctification, without which no one shall see the Lord (Hebrews 12; Titus 2; II Timothy 3).

This disciplining of the children of God in the world is however in reality, not a punishment for sin but rather a reward for doing righteousness (I Peter 2), a sign of the love of God and, at the same time, a means of purification and preservation from sin. The more wholly we have the life of Christ in us, the more deeply we shall be humiliated with Him in this world and the higher we stand in the grace of God. For we must humble ourselves under the mighty hand of God, that He may exalt us in due time, and we are not permitted to strive against the suffering and chastisements of this time, but should rejoice thereover and thank the Father for the correction (Matthew 5), for the sake of the precious fruit at the manifestation of His children, although it may not now seem exactly like joy to us, but rather sorrow. For it is better to bear a timely judgment than an eternal one.

It is not possible for us to endure rest in the flesh: we at once become indulgent, unrestrained, wilful and devious; we no longer cleanse ourselves from sin and follow after holiness. Even Paul had to have Satan's angel, lest he be overweening, and when he besought the Lord to be excused from him the answer was "My grace is sufficient for thee: for my strength is made perfect in weakness." Therefore he was willing to be weak in order to be strong and to boast in the Lord. Is His grace now sufficient for us and are we satisfied with it if we are children of God?

Will we let all things that God decrees for us please us for its sake?

There indeed are still other chastening rods for the children of God—not for the contented but for the discontented ones—and punishment for the committed deviations and defilement caused by inattention to the inner discipline of the Spirit, but even this outward correction is the love of God done for the purpose of purifying us that we may not be condemned with the world (I Corinthians 11:32).

> "But when we are judged, we are chastened
> of the Lord, that we should not be condemned
> with the world."

But he is no child of God who experiences neither the inward nor the outward chastening: God lets him go his own way and he is spared until the eternal judgment.

Chapter LV

The Glory Within

January 1, 1841 (Friday); Afternoon Meeting

From all that has been said, it might seem as if the imitation of Christ had nothing inviting or enjoyable about it, and with respect to the real Christian, from an outward aspect, it is true, he appears to be very lowly in this world, and anyone who considers the visible, finds that there is no advantage to be reaped and hence is frightened away. But the glory of the children of God is within and is hidden until Christ Himself, Who is their life, is revealed, when they also will be revealed in glory with Him (Romans 8; Colossians 3:4) (below), and indeed in such glory that the suffering of this time and all the glory of this world is to be considered as nothing.

> "When Christ, who is our life, shall appear,
> then shall ye also appear with him in glory."

For the present world with its lust, enjoyment and possessions is expedient for fallen men only, not for the children of God whose inheritance is kept in store in the future world and is still hidden with Christ.

The visible creation, on account of Adam's fall and of its misuse, now lies under the curse and the service of vanity and the perishable, not voluntarily but by force, in the hope however of its once-to-come liberation from bondage and, as such, it again reacts ruinously upon fallen man and is the lure and snare by which the devil draws men to destruction and condemnation.

It is the sign of true conversion if the mind and striving of a person is changed entirely, turned away from the visible and toward the invisible, and his own battle of faith consists in the denial and sacrifice of the transitory present and the earthly. For as Christ was a stranger in this world and only passed through without having anything of His own here or seeking it, so are the children of God also. It is true that they too use earthly things according to necessity, but they do not misuse them for idolatry or for the gratification of lust, for the earthly mind (covetousness, etc.) is the root of all evil. All the sins of men (murder, adultery, thievery, etc.) flow from this fountainhead.

But if the present world with its sham possessions appears so desirable to carnal men, how much more must the future world with its glory be thus to the spiritual, to the saints and children of God, where all things will be transposed into the original glorious estate of Paradise, as is befitting men who have been recovered in Christ.

For, as by Adam's fall a twofold destruction took place —in man and in the entire creation on account of man, so through Christ a twofold restoration takes place, first of man, inwardly, in those to whom the kingdom of God is appointed and after they all shall have entered in (in Christ), then Christ also appears again—in glory—and with that the whole creation is released anew from the curse of Adam's sin, under which it, until now, groans, together with the children of God.

This is now the hope of the saints that will be fulfilled in the first resurrection, in order that they renounce the present visible world which lies in wickedness, and on account of which they are looked upon as fools, since nothing has value for carnal men except that which they can see with their eyes, examine with their hands and enjoy with their sacrilegious mind; and yet there is nothing in the whole world that is good for us except the grace of Christ and the communion of His Spirit.

January 3, 1841 (Sunday) ; Morning Meeting
I John 3 : 3 and 4

> "And every man that hath this hope in him purifieth himself, even as he is pure.
> "Whosoever committeth sin transgresseth also the law: for sin is the transgression of the law."

The repeated "whosoever" shows that it concerns each individual person and that no one can, unworthily, by permission of the great masses, merely slink into the church with them. To be of the body of Christ, each member must be qualified for it, i.e., he must be holy. In the world no attention at all is paid to this. Each member of the body must accommodate himself to the Head and be minded as He is.

But we are still in the world and have not yet laid hold upon the goal of the calling, and *by practice* must first become like Jesus was (Philippians 3). Therefore we must watch and pray at all times so as to become qualified and worthy, for we are not saved unconditionally but upon the condition that we preserve the received grace of God and purify ourselves from sin because Christ is pure. For Christ has never sinned and cannot sin and *being in Him* is not sin; i.e., if we are in Him and abide in Him, then *we* cannot sin for only the devil sins, and whoever is not in Christ to do righteousness is in the devil to commit sin (II Peter 1).

Therefore, it depends upon our abiding in Christ, that we may be preserved until the end, unto blessedness, for the devil and his host is not removed by Christ's death but is overcome—bound—only for the believers in Christ, that they need no longer do his bidding. But he is still in the world (in the unbelievers) and reigns as before and, where possible, since Christ, to an even greater extent because abiding in the devil's power is a free choice and also a voluntary denial of Christ, and the believers themselves are enabled to remain free from him insofar only as they do not serve the lusts (sin), wherewith he has corrupted all in their nature and would like to corrupt those again who are saved in Christ, and if we are asleep it will happen all too soon.

But if God already demanded of the *unpardoned under the law* that they should guard themselves against transgression of the law (and that is not impossible even though it was given to the ungodly and sinners: for one can live and still be a sinner in Adam who has to let himself be helped by Christ without exactly being a murderer, an adulterer, a thief and the like) and since each such unnatural sin has received its just reward, recompense and punishment (Hebrews 2 and 10), how much more does He expect of the *pardoned in Christ* that they should keep themselves from new sins and defilement after they shall have died to sin itself, in Christ, and have been purified! Now, he who has a firm hope of the true glory must *purify himself here* from every defilement of the flesh and the spirit and perfect his holiness in the fear of God.

It is true that here below impure members may be found in the membership who do not really belong in it, even though they are not exactly adulterers, thieves, drunkards, blasphemers, robbers, and the like, but live orderly according to the law. But that does not suffice for the kingdom and the righteousness of God, and although we cannot here put them out from among us, they can nevertheless not enter into the kingdom of God because they are not *holy*. But if the state church were not entirely a Babel and a whore, she would *at least* have to put out those from her that live in open sins against the old law, for they are not even the tares of the field (Matthew 13), but in the state church itself is fulfilled what Christ says in Matthew 12:43 ff.:

> "When the unclean spirit is gone out of a man, he walketh through dry places, seeking rest, and findeth none.
>
> "Then he saith, I will return into my house from whence I came out; and when he is come, he findeth it empty, swept, and garnished.
>
> "Then goeth he, and taketh with himself seven other spirits more wicked than himself, and they enter in and dwell there: and the last state of that man is worse than the first.

Even so shall it be also unto this wicked generation."

The nominal Christians are worse than the heathen; and whoever will take his chance with them, let him still be and remain impure, filthy and unjust (Revelation 22:11).

"He that is unjust, let him be unjust still: and he which is filthy, let him be filthy still: and he that is righteous, let him be righteous still: and he that is holy, let him be holy still."

Chapter LVI

The Lively Hope of Future Glory

January 3, 1841 (Sunday); Afternoon Meeting
I John 3: 3 ff.

"And every man that hath this hope in him purifieth himself, even as he is pure.

"Whosoever committeth sin transgresseth also the law: for sin is the transgression of the law.

"And ye know that he was manifested to take away our sins; and in him is no sin.

"Whosoever abideth in him sinneth not: whosoever sinneth hath not seen him, neither known him.

"Little children, let no man deceive you: he that doeth righteousness is righteous, even as he is righteous.

"He that committeth sin is of the devil; for the devil sinneth from the beginning. For this purpose the Son of God was manifested, that he might destroy the works of the devil."

John places two things side by side, which *in the chil-*

dren of God are necessarily and inseparably allied to each other; namely, a lively hope of the future glory with Christ and a complete purification of oneself, so that no one may deceive himself with the false, imaginary hope that the hypocrites are deceived with, who have neither the ground, nor the seal, nor the pledge for it in them, because hope has to do with something invisible and future (Romans 8) and in the end he who has no divine security for it in him through the Holy Ghost is the one who is deceived.

Because the required purification refers to sin, it is evident that this demand is not made upon unconverted men, since natural man, as a born sinner, cannot purify or keep himself from sin. Only the believer and spiritual man in Christ is able to do that. The unconverted man, as a corrupt tree, can bear nothing except evil fruit; hence the reborn man, according to his nature, can bear nothing except good fruit because, in Christ, he has become a good tree. If, in this, the natural man would excuse himself with the impossibility of purifying himself and of living without sin, he would indeed be right; but that he cannot do so is his own fault because he remains willingly in Adam—in sin and in the devil—and does not let himself be released by Christ so as to live a holy life in Him. For the Son of God has come into the world for this, that He might destroy the works of the devil and rescue us from his power, if we become converted to Him and believe.

It is, to be sure, not man himself who could live without sin but it must be Christ in us Who can and does do it. For all sin is contrary to Christ's nature, and if we are in Him and abide in Him, we do not and cannot sin (it is an inner impossibility with the children of God, not an outer one, for if they do not keep themselves in Christ, they too can and must sin again). God and the devil do not dwell together in *one* heart; where one is, there the other must yield. Therefore it depends upon whom we belong to, whether to God in Christ or to the devil in Adam. For just as Adam is the ancestor of carnal man, so Christ is the Ancestor of the spiritual one.

But as soon as we are children of God, the devil and the world strive against us with every kind of temptation for apostasy from the Way of Life and under these circumstances, it is necessary that there be no longer any conception of sin in us, so that we may not lust after the evil as did Adam and the Old Israelites (I Corinthians 10). For indeed Jesus "was in all points tempted like as we are," but (unlike Adam) He did not enter into temptation but resisted out of love to the Father, and in temptation we shall imitate or follow Christ, not Adam. And Adam really sinned without necessity, but we come into such circumstances that we, so to speak, should sin of necessity, and if we cling to the visible and fall into unbelief, we fall into temptation and deny God, as if He would let us perish on the way when He at the same time holds out the goal of salvation before us, and if we always look toward this goal in faith we will allow nothing to separate us from the love of God (Romans 8: 35 ff.).

> "Who shall separate us from the love of Christ? shall tribulation, or distress, or persecution, or famine, or nakedness, or peril, or sword?
> "As it is written, For thy sake we are killed all the day long; we are accounted as sheep for the slaughter.
> "Nay, in all these things we are more than conquerors through him that loved us.
> "For I am persuaded, that neither death, nor life, nor angels, nor principalities, nor

powers, nor things present, nor things to come,

> "Nor height, nor depth, nor any other creature, shall be able to separate us from the love of God, which is in Christ Jesus our Lord."

But that requires the great conflict, which is difficult indeed, because it has to do with offering up all that is earthly and visible, and only to the overcomers is the inheritance promised (Revelation 21:7; Hebrews 10:32 ff.).

> "He that overcometh shall inherit all things; and I will be his God, and he shall be my son."

> "But call to remembrance the former days, in which, after ye were illuminated, ye endured a great fight of afflictions;
>
> "Partly, whilst ye were made a gazingstock both by reproaches and afflictions; and partly, whilst ye became companions of them that were so used.
>
> "For ye had compassion of me in my bonds, and took joyfully the spoiling of your goods, knowing in yourselves that ye have in heaven a better and an enduring substance."

Where the heart was purified rightly in the beginning, there keeping it so afterwards is an easy matter; but where this has not occurred, there the house does not stand in temptation (Matthew 7) because it does not come to doing the will of God and the seed does not bring forth fruit unto eternal life (Matthew 13), but the devil through love of the earthly becomes master again. For in every case temptation comes and the devil says, "In this world I am the Lord and he who will not serve me shall have no share in it."

CHAPTER LVII

THE PURPOSE OF PREPARING OURSELVES

January 5, 1841 (Tuesday) ; Evening Meeting
I John 3 : 3

"And every man that hath this hope in him
purifieth himself, even as he is pure."

It is to be noted that John does not say, "And every
man that hath this hope in him *shall* purify himself," but
"*purifieth* himself." It is not an outer command, but an
inner impulse of the Spirit of Christ in the children of
God, for the very reason that they have the hope of glory
as the goal toward which they press, that they may reach
it. For every impurity and defilement that makes us unfit
for entry into the kingdom must *here* and *now* have been
put aside, seeing that anything which carries any defilement with it remains on one, and purity is not an impossible thing with those who have once been cleansed
(washed) in the blood of Christ of all their former sins.
They shall merely *preserve* what they have received, and
everyone who has actually been purified has, through
that, at the same time, received the strength and ability
of the Spirit to guard himself from new defilement.

Otherwise the cleansing in the blood of Christ would
be useless, if it made no difference whether we defiled
ourselves again afterwards, and if baptism were only the
purification of our former sins and would not, at the same
time, offer the strength and protection against new ones,
it would, of course, be best that we saved baptism until
the end of life (as was once the custom). Then, least of all,
should we baptize little children at the beginning of life.

However, the main thing about baptism is precisely this ensuing power of the life of Christ, since Christ does not come with water alone but with water and blood and Spirit, because no one can be saved as a sinner but only as a saint, or Christ would have come and died in vain and a new birth from the kingdom of God would be superfluous. But John says exactly the opposite: Christ was manifested to take away—put an end to, abolish—our sin, as the Lamb of God, and in him is no sin, so that anyone who is in Him and abides in Him does not sin either, but the devil—and whoever is in him and abides in him—sins.

But sin and its purification is the least thing that man troubles himself about (for what?), for they too expect to be saved as sinners and children of the devil, and strive only for that which is of this world because they do not realize the purpose of their being here or of their life. Our lifetime on earth is given, granted and meted out to us by God, only for this, that we should prepare ourselves for the revelation of His Kingdom by purifying and sanctifying ourselves, even as Christ the High Priest is pure and holy and without sin, so that we may become first-fruits of the creatures of God and belong to the church of the Firstborn, who are written in heaven. Therefore John uses the same word here as in John 11:55:

> "And the Jews' passover was nigh at hand: and many went out of the country up to Jerusalem before the passover, to purify themselves."

Just as the Israelites were required to purify themselves before the Feast of the Passover so that they could be pronounced levitically pure to eat the paschal lamb, so has the time following our conversion been appointed to us, that we should purify ourselves for entering into the holy place as priests of God (Revelation 20). For all who will attain to the Millennium of Christ must be saints who have not stained their garments, or have not loved their life in this world, even unto death, but who have resisted unto blood in the struggle against sin (Hebrews 12:4).

> "Ye have not yet resisted unto blood, striving against sin."

So that we may not be provoked or allured by the perishable lusts of this world to apostasy of the heart from Christ, we must put every restraint upon ourselves and not spare our right eye or our right hand that would mislead us into sin (Matthew 5:29; Mark 9:43 ff.).

> "And if thy right eye offend thee, pluck it out, and cast it from thee: for it is profitable for thee that one of thy members should perish, and not that thy whole body should be cast into hell."

> "And if thy hand offend thee, cut it off: it is better for thee to enter into life maimed, than having two hands to go into hell, into the fire that never shall be quenched:
> "Where their worm dieth not, and the fire is not quenched.
> "And if thy foot offend thee, cut it off: it is better for thee to enter halt into life, than having two feet to be cast into hell, into the fire that never shall be quenched:
> "Where their worm dieth not, and the fire is not quenched.
> "And if thine eye offend thee, pluck it out: it is better for thee to enter into the kingdom

of God with one eye, than having two eyes to
be cast into hell fire:

"Where their worm dieth not, and the fire
is quenched."

Here we shall guard ourselves most against the first defilement, because one likes best to keep a clean garment
clean and does not mind so much soiling anew an already
soiled garment.

January 7, 1841 (Thursday); Evening Meeting
I John 3:4

"Whosoever committeth sin transgresseth
also the law: for sin is the transgression of
the law."

The opposite of purity and the purification of oneself
is the committing of sin, and sin is everything that defiles
and disfigures the inner man and that does not let itself
be reconciled with the divine "light" nature. Therefore
a child of God considers no sin insignificant, but then it
depends upon the inner situation and degree of enlightenment, which is not equally great in all, to see and to
recognize sin.

The first step of enlightenment takes place under the
law for recognition of one's committed sins and of one's
own perdition and condemnation in sin. Here God Himself speaks with the voice of thunder from Sinai to the
frightened sinners, who are so greatly horrified by this
vision that they hide themselves, and say: "Speak thou
[Moses] with us, and we will hear: but let not God speak
with us, lest we die." And God says, "They have well
spoken that which they have spoken," that He will raise
up another Prophet, in Moses' stead, Who will speak to
them in His name, and the soul that will not hearken
unto *this* Prophet shall die.

It is, therefore, not Moses, neither is it John the Baptist, who grants us the real salvation and redemption, but it is Christ the Son, Whom we shall hear, after we, by the first voice, have come to the knowledge of sin and condemnation, and only then, in Christ, does the real light of life appear for us. Further, the sinner would not be able to endure for any length of time the terrifying light of the law and its curse: he would have to despair; and actually the law has no abiding provision but only a passing one and when it has accomplished its work, it must cease and make room for the Gospel of Christ in all those contrite and anxious hearts so that they may receive grace and peace, soundness and strength in Christ.

But then there is a class of men who put the wrong interpretation upon this intention of the law and, instead of allowing themselves to be condemned by the same, take this sting from it, set up a righteousness of their own of works of the law (against the righteousness of God in Christ), compose and settle themselves in it; boast and imagine that they had comprehended it and are believing children of God because they can prattle about sin and grace, the law and the Gospel; they would, at the same time, be poor sinners and children of God, ungodly and righteous, i.e., would at the same time be under the law and under grace, but they are under neither, but are untoward hypocrites who are not concerned about the healing of their hurt in Adam. For he who has been under the law rightly cannot always remain thereunder but instead must come under the grace in Christ so as to be healed and freed from sin, for Christ indeed is a Physician; however not such a one who would let the sick remain in their infirmities, but One Who heals them thoroughly so that they need not sin any more thereafter.

Yet the hypocrites say that it is not possible for man to

live without sin, and that is why Christ cannot heal them; they are a cross between the entirely gross sinners (who are insensible to sin) and the real children of God who, at one and the same time, have become free from the law and from sin. The hypocrites think that Christ did not lift off the curse of the law for us, but that sin itself was removed, and therefore they are worse and more condemnable in the sight of God than all other sinners—because they want to be in a place between the two.

Chapter LVIII

Inner and Perfect Enlightenment

January 10, 1841 (Sunday); Morning Meeting
I John 3 : 4 ff.

"Whosoever committeth sin transgresseth also the law: for sin is the transgression of the law.

"And ye know that he was manifested to take away our sins; and in him is no sin.

"Whosoever abideth in him sinneth not: whosoever sinneth hath not seen him, neither known him.

"Little children, let no man deceive you: he that doeth righteousness is righteous, even as he is righteous.

"He that committeth sin is of the devil; for the devil sinneth from the beginning. For this purpose the Son of God was manifested, that he might destroy the works of the devil.

"Whosoever is born of God doth not commit sin; for his seed remaineth in him: and he cannot sin, because he is born of God.

"In this the children of God are manifest,

and the children of the devil: whosoever doeth not righteousness is not of God, neither he that loveth not his brother."

John makes the mounting distinction between *sin* in general and *transgression of the law*. The former is the *nature-sin* (in Adam), committed in *ignorance;* the latter however is *unnatural* sin, for where a definite law has been transgressed, there one cannot excuse himself with ignorance. Paul says (Romans 7: 7b) : "I had not known lust, except the law had said, Thou shalt not covet [desire another's good]." For the root of the sin-deed is *lusting* and therefore *that* must already be recognized and combated *as sin* so that it may not become a deed (as transgression of the law). Sin itself is already threatening in the lust of it, but only as a born deed-*sin* is it *condemnable*. The law however is also discriminating according to the circumstance.

Under the Old Testament where man is a sinner by nature, the law is negative and forbids only *unnatural* sin and if he to whom the law is given commits such sin, he is condemned by the letter of the law, whereas for the heathen who commits the *same* sin, and that without excuse because he has the law within himself (Romans 1 and 2), it, consequently, is unnatural sin also, but yet he is less punishable than the Jew who, with the inner law of nature, has the outer letter as well, which makes sin a conscience matter [convicts him] (II Corinthians 3) and, by that, it is made condemnable and kills him (serves him unto death).

Under the New Testament in Christ however, man is no longer a born nature-sinner but a born, natural child of God—holy, righteous—and, as such, works righteously and fulfils all righteousness: for the former sin is gone and in Christ there is none. It is for this reason that the positive law of the Spirit—love to God and man—has, accordingly, been given to him, that he shall keep it inviolably and for this higher state of grace and truth in Christ, this demand is not greater than the old law is for the old man (which forbids only unnatural sins and, besides, does not demand positive justice).

That is why he who might have kept the whole law, like the rich young man (Matthew 19), is still a sinner before God, and Christ says to him: "If thou wilt be perfect, go and sell that thou hast, and give to the poor, and thou shalt have treasure in heaven: and come and follow me." This perfection therefore is a state of the children of God, who, in Christ, are no longer sinners but saints, and lies in the new law of love, which, for just that reason, is not as limited and conditional as the love of the nature-man but is unlimited and unconditional like the love of God (Matthew 5), which does not recompense evil for evil and good for good, but good for evil (Romans 13).

Just as *unnatural* sin was forbidden by the law in the Old Testament, beside which much natural sin still remained so that man could not become pure and perfect before God, so, on the other hand, by the commandment of the New Testament, is *natural* sin forbidden and to be avoided and, consequently, complete purification is *possible;* but because the new law is positive (demands the doing of righteousness), the transgressing of this law —i.e., the failure to do the good, acceptable and perfect will of God (love to our neighbor)—is also a sin. The doing of the opposing evil however (which is not expressly forbidden therein) shall no longer be even heard of among the saints (children of God) (Ephesians 4 and 5), lest we go back under the old law of condemnation: for love does no evil to one's neighbor and therefore love is the fulfilment of the law and all is summed up into *one* commandment.

But the more perfect the inner enlightenment is, the better also every inner deviation from the holy rule is recognized, and love (or enmity) towards men is but the outer mark of the inner state from and to God. For he who fulfils his duty to God (loves God) fulfils it also to men and the commandment of love to one's neighbor, actually, is already comprised in the commandment of the love of God, as in this one commandment of the New Testament the entire Old Testament is included (Matthew 22).

Our inner law in Christ is set much higher than the old one was (Matthew 5), since it is given for the inwardly concealed man of the heart; accordingly, no one can judge us except God Himself, Who tries the heart and reins. Therefore Christ says, "Ye have heard that it was said by them of old time, Thou shalt not kill, [etc.]. But I say unto you,"—that your heart and mind must be pure and perfect, and then your outward life of itself will be pure. But here there can still be deviation from the holy rule (by omission of the good), without one's being exactly removed from the state of perfection, but a child of God shall purify himself even of that; it is also possible that love may sometimes overlook something without evil intention.

January 10, 1841 (Sunday); Afternoon Meeting

In the New Testament (i.e., in Christ), the law is *love or the doing of righteousness;* consequently in it absence of love (uncharitableness and unkindness) is then sin, for we owe love to all (Romans 13). "Therefore to him that knoweth to do good, and doeth it not, to him it is sin (James 4:17)." But he who does not do the good, certainly just as easily does the opposite—evil. For a child of God however, the doing of righteousness is just as *natural* as the committing of sin is for a child of the devil, and if a child of God does not do the good he denies his nature and origin from God.

The new law of the Spirit is given to the *new* man in Christ just as the old law of the flesh was given to the old man in Adam (because, in it, man is still carnal and sold under sin), and as the sinner commits sin, so the righteous man does righteousness: i.e., a man is a sinner before he commits sin, or he commits sin because he is a sinner, not *vice versa*. Thus also must a man first be righteous in Christ before he is able to do righteousness, and he is a righteous man not by reason of his doing righteousness, but he does righteousness because he has become a righteous man. By the fruit the tree is known.

The hypocrites reverse this and will be righteous and saved because of the good they imagine they have done. In this way however, no one will be saved for that is not the new way in Christ, but the one of the old world of nature and of the law. When the children of God thus do all righteousness, they seek neither renown nor reward for themselves because of it, for it is God's grace and gift in Christ which enables them to do righteousness and by it they merely reveal their divine nature. For if they do not do the good, they sin by omission of their duty; and if they have done all that has been commanded to them, they still have no overage, for Christ says: "Plant this corrupt tree and the fruit also will be evil." Or, "Plant this good tree and the fruit also will be good."

But even though a child of God loves all men without exception—not only his friends but his enemies as well, he nevertheless does not love all alike or without making a distinction: for with genuine love toward our fellow men, hatred and wrath for sin is also allied because we know that sin is the destruction of men; therefore we do not love them if we silently let them perish. God has indeed demonstrated His pure, sincere love for the ungodly, lost sinner-world for "He gave his only begotten Son, that whosoever believeth in him should not perish, but have everlasting life." Yet right in this greatest proof of His love, we at the same time see His ill-will and wrath over sin, on account of which men would have to be separated from God eternally. However, he who does not now avail himself of the love of God that is manifested in Christ, so as to let himself be purified from sin and saved from the power of Satan by Christ's death on the cross, will afterwards, at the second appearance of Christ (Acts 17: 30), still encounter the wrath of God.

> "And the times of this ignorance God winked at; but now commandeth all men every where to repent:"

Concerning our love of our fellow men, the world, which is surely very selfish and partial in *its* love, reproves the children of God for uncharitableness because they do not regard all men in a like manner, as brethren in Christ, but witness that the world in its sin and unrighteousness is not of God but of the devil and therefore cannot come to God and be saved. Just as God loves His own children (namely as a father) in a way that is different from the way in which He loves the world, so the children of God also make a distinction in their love of their brethren in Christ and their love of all other men, although they love these too and seek to save them, even in spite of the world's hatred, and sacrifice their own life because they look to the end and the judgment.

For although Christ came the first time as a Savior of

the World, to reconcile the world to God and to save the lost, He will still come the second time as a Judge of the World and as an Avenger of Disobedience and a Rewarder of Obedience, and then will separate, right and left, the sheep from the goats, and although the goats are of the same generation (race, i.e., according to name they are Christians too) that the sheep are of, the lot and judgment of the two nevertheless will be entirely different, for to those at His left He will say: "Depart from me, ye cursed, into everlasting fire, prepared for the devil and his angels."

And why?—It is indeed terrible to hear. Not because they have been thieves, murderers, adulterers and the like, but because they have *not* done the good—have not served Him in charity in the least of His brethren. "For I was an hungred, and ye gave me no meat," etc. Now if that is the measuring rod of the future judgment, we can easily conclude on which side the greater number will stand: those who have or those who have not done this! Therefore the enlightened and prudent children of God follow the rule:

"And whatsoever ye do, do it heartily, as to the Lord, and not unto men;
"Knowing that of the Lord ye shall receive the reward of the inheritance: for ye serve the Lord Christ."

—Colossians 3:23, 24

CHAPTER LIX

THE SUFFERINGS OF THE CHILDREN OF GOD

January 12, 1841 (Tuesday) ; Evening Meeting
I John 3 : 4

The new law and the old, in their propriety and nature, are completely different: for while the latter forbids only the evil and is outward, the former is inward, written in the heart and, through love, urges the doing of all the good, acceptable and perfect will of God which, in itself, is voluntary and cannot be forced by the rod. He who does the evil from habit, certainly does not do the good; but he who is able to do the good, likewise does not do the evil, for only in the doing of righteousness does true blessedness, his designation of God and his likeness to Him, lie. All evil painfully grieves a child of God as it is entirely against the nature and the will of God and is unbecoming to man, who has been created in the image of God. Only the good is fitting to the dignity and designation of man: for sin, as the nature of the devil, has merely been appended and does really not belong to man at all.

For this, the Son of God has come, that He might take sin away from us and destroy the work of the devil and as soon as one is in Christ, the doing of righteousness is just as easy for him and as natural to him as the committing of sin is for the children of the devil, although the liars and hypocrites deny that man could attain thereto, i.e., be without sin—live righteously and holy and godly in this world—because they prefer darkness to light and pass Christ by as an object of aversion, as did the priest and the Levite (Luke 10: 31 and 32).

"And by chance there came down a certain priest that way: and when he saw him, he passed by on the other side.

"And likewise a Levite, when he was at the place, came and looked on him, and passed by on the other side."

And as our nature, since Adam's fall, commands us to cover our body to hide our nakedness and shame (and no one would like to be unclothed before the people), so the sinner seeks darkness for his evil works and to hide under because he does not know and fear the living God. But God will once uncover them in all their malice and darkness, and they will have to be revealed in all their shame, nakedness and destitution because they preferred to be unenlightened by Christ in this life and not to become, from children of the devil, children of God and thus attain to their true, divine destiny. Because the love of God shed abroad in the heart is the nature of all children of God, their love and the doing of good is one and the same thing and therein consists the fulfilment of the new law and the old one, simultaneously. Therefore, not to love (not to do the good) is the nonfulfilment of the law and is sin, and from there to hatred is but a short step.

January 14, 1841 (Thursday); Evening Meeting
I John 3 : 4 ff.

With Christ and the Gospel, it is a matter of sin and righteousness only. Sin is all that strives against the nature and good will of God, for which reason all children of God must be purified from it and that is their only difference from the children of the devil, that the latter commit sin the while the former lay aside everything they recognize as sin in the light of the truth of God because they are in Christ and no longer in Adam, for by his saying, "in him is no sin," John does not mean it in reference to the person of Christ but in reference to *us*, inasmuch as we are new men of God in Christ, created in Him unto good works.

In this new state of grace, sin, as the kingdom of the devil, has come to an end for it cannot exist along with the kingdom of God (I Peter 4:1);

"Forasmuch then as Christ hath suffered
for us in the flesh, arm yourselves likewise
with the same mind: for he that hath suffered
in the flesh hath ceased from sin;"

yet the devil's outer might has not ended with his inner might, and so he persecutes and plagues with tribulations the children of God all the more in the flesh because he can no longer get at them from within. But the sufferings of the children of God have an entirely different character from the sufferings of the children of the devil; the former endure them innocently and without resistance for the sake of God and His righteousness and therefore they also have the blessing of them in sanctification, for they must endure their judgment *in this world* because of the wrath of the devil and the world. Sinners by their sins however, even now, have and cause themselves affliction in the flesh, but they do not bear it willingly, nor is it a blessing to them but instead a punishment from God by reason of sin.

And if poor humanity should notice by nothing else that the devil reigns over them through sin, they should feel it in their countless sorrows as the direct result of sin, with which the whole world is filled, and in this respect, these sorrows themselves, upon authority of the will of God, should be beneficent for they bring men to the knowledge of their misery and impel them to conversion from sin and the power of Satan. But this good intention is attained only upon the fewest, and therefore even their sufferings are a curse and a foretaste of eternal judgment to them rather than a blessing; so far is it removed that the afflictions of the unbelievers would be a cross as the afflictions of the believers are an honor before God and a foretoken of the future glory (Philippians 1:28 ff.; II Thessalonians 3:1).

> "And in nothing terrified by your adversaries: which is to them an evident token of perdition, but to you of salvation, and that of God.
> "For unto you it is given in the behalf of Christ, not only to believe on him, but also to suffer for his sake;
> "Having the same conflict which ye saw in me, and now hear to be in me."

> "Finally, brethren, pray for us, that the word of the Lord may have free course, and be glorified, even as it is with you:"

Had Adam not sinned, one would know nothing of sorrow and the time is coming in the Paradise of God when the children of God shall be released outwardly also from all their sufferings in the flesh (Revelation 21:4).

> "And God shall wipe away all tears from their eyes; and there shall be no more death, neither sorrow, nor crying, neither shall there be any more pain: for the former things are passed away."

January 17, 1841 (Sunday); Morning Meeting
I John 3:5 and 6

"And ye know that he was manifested to take away our sins; and in him is no sin.

"Whosoever abideth in him sinneth not: whosoever sinneth hath not seen him, neither known him."

"Whosoever abideth in him sinneth not:" This abiding in Christ is here to be understood not as an *enduring* to the end (according to time), but as a constant, unabstracted *clinging* to Christ in the *Spirit,* by which we are one (one Spirit) with Him; foster a continuous association with Him, learn of Him and put on His mind. It is the opposite of our mind in Adam as sinners, and one, like the other, has come to pass in the two authors, of *salvation* and of *harm,* and is our portion without our assistance—death and sin through our birth from Adam, righteousness and life through our new birth from God. For when Adam sinned, he was still alone and yet all his descendants have inherited death from him and are *sinners* by nature, although they have not sinned by the same transgression as he has; and when Christ died in Adam's stead and by His death abolished the death in Adam, He also was still alone, and yet all who should inherit salvation were included and comprised in Him.

And although not all the fallen and dead in Adam have been raised up anew and made alive in Christ (because not all believe), yet salvation comes in the same way as harm, namely as a gift and an inheritance, and whoever does not acquire salvation in the same way as he received the harm in Adam, has himself to blame because he does not accept it as a free gift of the grace of God but prefers to remain a sinner in Adam rather than to become a righteous man and son of God in Christ. Thus the choice of death (in Adam) and of life (in Christ) is optional to everyone who hears the Gospel and contempt of this proffered salvation draws condemnation upon it; and although the harm is first, yet Adam is not mightier than Christ, Who has won our salvation and desires to give it to us.

But in order that we may not continue to be children of the devil in Adam but may become children of God in Christ, sin (death) must be separated from us (as husband and wife are separated in wedlock by death), that we may belong to Christ *the Risen One,* and by our union with Him bring forth fruit unto God in righteousness; i.e., be in Christ as He through His Spirit is in us and lives. Then abiding in Him is not a troublesome, forced, affected remembering of Him, but after we have recognized the gift of God and have prayed for it to Him Who stands before us in His Word, He gives us His living water, which then becomes a living fountain in us and flows on into eternal life (John 4).

Chapter LX

Contentment in the Spirit

In an inner alliance and fellowship with the Father and the Son lies the only real contentment of our spirit and longing, whereas in all the enjoyment of the sham- and shadow-good of this world, no genuine satisfaction obtains, only deception and illusion: the more one has and enjoys, the more he desires to have; he ever thirsts anew. But the beginning of the realistic in children of God awakens with an unquenchable longing and yearning for the Upper Fatherland and in *this* world they feel strange and uncomfortable, like captives in hope of release. This homesickness for that which is above is wanting in the children of this world and, by it, one recognizes who is a

Christian, and realizes that it is not possible to abide in Christ and at the same time commit sin; and when temptations to sin arise, a child of God overcomes them by love to Christ.

Now if anyone should find that this is not the case with him and he is frightened, let him know that God's Word stands firm against the lie of men, and let him not be satisfied with the condition under the law, but let him seek in Christ to become what he not yet is. —Carnal men with respect to the physical life say that one cannot live on air; one must have something to bite and chew. Thus it is also with the real, spiritual life in Christ. No one can be a Christian in fancy only and live in the Spirit: Christ must actually exist in a Christian and must really be partaken of. The carnal minded do not understand this and therefore they are content with an idle wind and word.

January 17, 1841 (Sunday); Afternoon Meeting

If we are children of God in Christ, we must have a righteousness of life that proves effectual, not only before men but before God Himself, and that may stand stedfast; i.e., not a mere *external*, human uprightness but an inner and a divine purity of heart and mind. An unconverted person can, it is true, appropriate a human righteousness (according to the law) to himself, so that one can lay nothing against him before men and this accordingly commands respect in the world. Therefore the Pharisee ranks highest in this; but because the Pharisees are hypocrites, their righteousness is without merit in the sight of God, Who looks upon the hearts, not upon the outward appearance as do men. And if our righteousness of life does not surpass that of the Pharisees and scribes *inwardly,* we cannot enter into the kingdom of God. But such righteousness that is recognized as good before God, is not human but superhuman and divine, and excels all human effort by far. Only in Christ is it granted to us and indeed not by mere imputation of His righteousness through faith, but by actual fulfillment of the same in us (Romans 8; Ephesians 1:4), that we no longer walk according to the flesh but according to the Spirit.

> "According as he hath chosen us in him before the foundation of the world, that we should be holy and without blame before him in love:"

In this respect, there are only children of God and children of the devil; in the former the living God dwells and works by His Spirit (John 4), in the latter however the devil by the spirit of the world (I Corinthians 2; II Corinthians 4); in the former God has His good pleasure, even as in His Son, but the latter have no mind to please Him because they hate Christ and therefore the Father also.

The infallible proof, whether one is of God or of the devil, lies in the mind—in thought and endeavor—for although one cannot look into the heart of man, yet that which is within it is made manifest by his striving, whereby men betray themselves. Whosoever is of God seeks that which is of God: His kingdom, His righteousness, His good pleasure, His honor; but whosoever is of the devil, that which is of the world: pride, honor, riches, a life of pleasure in the flesh and just as mighty as the devil is in his children unto sin, so mighty is God also in His children unto righteousness. Inasmuch as John says, "Whosoever abideth in him sinneth not," the opposite, "Whosoever sinneth hath not seen him, neither known him," explains best what abiding in Christ means.

Thus, abiding in Christ is as much as seeing and knowing Christ and he who at all times sees and *consequently* knows Christ in the Spirit, does not and cannot sin; but because Christ Himself is now hidden and our life also with Him in God, if we are children of God, this is not a corporeal but a spiritual seeing and knowing, notwithstanding that He at all times has His children and witnesses in the world also, in whom He, as it were, is visibly and incarnately here and walks before men so that they may learn to know Him.

Since it is the duty of the children of God to represent Christ as faithfully and as perfectly as possible in His holy mind and righteous life, so that on their account His holy name may not be reviled, as in the case of the false Christians and Greeks of Laodicea, the world, which rejects its witnesses, sins not only against the visible witnesses but also against God Himself Who, by His Spirit, lives in His saints; and the spiritual can indeed understand and judge all other men, of which spirit they are children, but the carnal cannot judge or even recognize the children of God. But if those who openly confess Christ do not, in all respects, walk according to their confession, carnal men see and judge that too and the world clamors much more about a little stain in the company of the children of God than about the greatest sin of one of their own. This should teach us to live discreetly and inoffensively.

In the case of all men, we need only to observe what kind of *spirit is in them* (whether the spirit of the world or the Spirit of God), not what they are and appear to be according to the flesh (privileged or lowly), for the higher one stands in the flesh and in the world, the more right the devil has to him. But true, divine nobleness scorns spurious highness in this world and keeps itself in lowliness as did Christ. In carnal men one can also see the depth of their spirit, for when one of them dies they are no longer mindful of him; but one can clearly distinguish the Spirit of Christ from the *spirit of the world* and *Christ in us* with His righteousness is not known in and by the world for it is offensive to it.

Chapter LXI

The Purpose of Our Life

January 19, 1841 (Tuesday); Evening Meeting
I John 3 : 5 ff.

"And ye know that he was manifested to take away our sins; and in him is no sin.

"Whosoever abideth in him sinneth not: whosoever sinneth hath not seen him, neither known him.

"Little children, let no man deceive you: he that doeth righteousness is righteous, even as he is righteous.

"He that committeth sin is of the devil; for the devil sinneth from the beginning. For this purpose the Son of God was manifested, that he might destroy the works of the devil."

In reference to *not committing sin,* the apostle merely brings the sum total of the Gospel to the remembrance of the believers, "And ye know that he was manifested to take away our sins." This manifestation of the Son of God in the flesh stands in the closest kind of connection with our condition and necessity and, from it, we shall take our designation of God, that we think it must indeed be for a great, important purpose that God has sent His own *Son* into the world and made Him manifest in the flesh (Hebrews 2; I Timothy 3 : 16).

> "And without controversy great is the mystery of godliness: God was manifest in the flesh, justified in the Spirit, seen of angels, preached unto the Gentiles, believed on in the world, received up into glory."

—Because, without Him, we (as sinners) cannot attain to our designation of God, i.e., stand in eternal fellowship with God. When we consider that there is only *one* God Who has made all things and that among all His works, the earth where we live sinks into insignificance as a mere speck among the countless number of great heavenly bodies, we must indeed be overwhelmed in humble astonishment and exclaim with David (Psalm 8: 3 f.):

> "When I consider thy heavens, the work of thy fingers, the moon and the stars, which thou hast ordained;
> "What is man, that thou art mindful of him? and the son of man, that thou visitest him?"

Yet God has manifested and lowered Himself to us—men—in such an astounding way that the Presentation from the Father has appeared in our flesh and blood to die for our sin and to take it away from us in the same way in which it has penetrated to all men by the fall of Adam, in that He saved us anew from the power of Satan, the adversary of God and the murderer of men from the beginning, and translated us to fellowship with God by putting an end to the enmity against Him, namely, the disposition of the flesh, which is death. In this, all natural men in relation to God, are in the densest darkness and grope like the blind. They do not discern Him and feel how near He is (as a Spirit Who penetrates and searches all). They seek and love and worship and idolize only the earthly and in their unbelief think: If there is a God and a Creator, it is still too insignificant for Him to regard men personally and so deny the only true God (Psalm 10) and say in their hearts, "There is no God!"

And although God has manifested Himself through His own Son for our deliverance from this principality of darkness, yet even this does not bring about more faith but rather scorn and mockery and contempt; and the devil presents the salvation in Christ as being unnecessary for men. Especially in the last fifty years, has this spirit of unbelief and apostasy from Christ penetrated all classes and the hearts of men, that it seems ridiculous to them to believe in the Son of God to be redeemed from the power of Satan and to become reunited with God and so attain to their real designation, which now becomes the portion only of some, namely to ascend anew to fellowship with God through faith in Christ. For if in our ignorance and unenlightenment we should ask, "For what purpose really are we here?" the Word of God replies (Psalm 8: 5, 6a):

"For thou hast made him a little lower than the angels, and hast crowned him with glory and honour.
"Thou madest him to have dominion over the works of thy hands;"

The new man in Christ shall be the nearest to God; whereas, by the sin of Adam we have been made so low, have been so debased and so far removed from God that we cling to and honor the idolatrous,—that which is vain, sinful and unworthy of our love, and of which we must be ashamed as soon as we come to the knowledge of our exalted designation of God, that according to the will of God we should be raised above all His works, and this on the condition that we let ourselves be made free from sin through Christ. Then we possess the living God and in Him all things. But has Christ now accomplished the purpose of His manifestation in the flesh as far as we ourselves are concerned? Has he made *us* free from the power of Satan so that we might become children and heirs of God?

January 21, 1841 (Thursday) ; Evening Meeting
I John 3 : 5 ff.

> "And ye know that he was manifested [in the flesh] to take away our sins [make an end to sin] ;"

This is the real Gospel, about which the whole world should rightly rejoice, namely that through Christ the devil's kingdom in men should reach its termination and God's kingdom of righteousness and peace come in its stead (Luke 2:14; I Timothy 3:16).

> "Glory to God in the highest, and on earth peace, good will toward men."

> "And without controversy great is the mystery of godliness: God was manifest in the flesh, justified in the Spirit, seen of angels, preached unto the Gentiles, believed on in the world, received up into glory."

But there is little rejoicing among men over this good "little" message, and just as His own did not receive Him upon His appearance on earth, so it still happens to Him right along. Of such a Savior Who redeems us from sin and destroys the works of the devil, the world wishes to know nothing.

This living, veritable Christ is still regarded as a deceiver! And although the proclamation of the birth of the Son of God has pressed forward through the whole world and is still vastly rehearsed each year, it is still not believed. And yet He was manifested for this, that a decision be made about sin and enmity against God, and righteousness and peace be brought upon earth. Nevertheless men will joyfully serve sin (i.e., the devil) and will still be called Christians, although no sinners are of God but of the devil, and indeed as long as all are alike in this, one can see no difference between light and darkness.

But as soon as Christ appears with His Gospel and breaks through in some unto conversation and a new life from God, so soon does the devil awaken his children also (the liars, John 8:44) (below) to the most violent resistance and enmity against the light, that they become blindly zealous for their paternal position and persecute the children of God as new believers and sectarians.

> "Ye are of your father the devil, and the lusts of your father ye will do. He was a murderer from the beginning, and abode not in the truth, because there is no truth in him. When he speaketh a lie, he speaketh of his own: for he is a liar, and the father of it."

Therefore it is clear that Christ came into the world and died, not in order to leave men in sin and the power of Satan and in enmity against God, but in order to redeem them therefrom and to make peace.

But it is strange that as soon as the Gospel proves its saving and converting power in some and so attains its intention, dissension arises and the hidden enmity against God is revealed against God's children, as Christ said (Luke 12:51 f.).

> "Suppose ye that I am come to give peace on earth? I tell you, Nay; but rather division:
>
> "For from henceforth there shall be five in one house divided, three against two, and two against three."

Not that Christ makes this enmity, the devil makes it. But still the world blames the Gospel, so unknown is the real Christ in the world, although He has revealed Himself and therefore is no longer concealed. He is near to us in His Word, so that no one can excuse himself, as if one could not know Him. He reveals and declares Himself by His Spirit (Romans 10) to everyone who believes, so that anyone can see and know Him by His mind in all righteousness who will not permit himself to sin (even though it would not be revealed in this world)—now that the light of the presence of God goes before him.

January 24, 1841 (Sunday); Morning Meeting
I John 3:6

> "Whosoever abideth in him sinneth not: whosoever sinneth hath not seen him, neither known him."

Every person has the character which is engraved in him and which he can neither change nor deny because it is his nature. With the children of God it's righteousness, with the children of the devil it's sin, and even though the sinner knows ever so well how to disguise himself, it is still so far removed that hypocrisy should change his nature or deny his character, that there is much lying and dissembling in one's own artifice and in the real nature of the devil and his children (John 8:44; II Corinthians 11) because they hide their sins and wish to represent themselves better than they are.

> "Ye are of your father the devil, and the lusts of your father ye will do. He was a murderer from the beginning, and abode not in the truth, because there is no truth in him. When he speaketh a lie, he speaketh of his own: for he is a liar, and the father of it."

But children of God never do this. It is not necessary for them to put a cloak for malice over them for they are revealed before God, and true godliness is not merely patched up and painted on the outside, like the pretended piety of the hypocrites, but is deeply engraved within in children of God, as His nature. One must not let himself be blinded, mistaken, imposed upon and deceived by outward appearance. Children of the devil may disguise their real nature and way as much as they will, they still are not children of God and do not have upon them the seal, which is always the same, everywhere, and is stamped upon everything a man of God does.

Sin is ever in the children of the devil as the nature of their father and also comes forth, if one can observe them in their daily life without their masks, how full they are of unrighteousness, arrogance, pride, avarice, anger, strife, lust of the flesh, etc. Sin is in every person born and that is why by nature all are children of the devil, and the thoughts and endeavors of man are only evil from his youth upwards and through Christ the devilish nature should be uprooted and the divine implanted in its place. The old and the new, the devilish and the divine nature, cannot both be at the same time in man, and in the full liberty of the children of God there resides the avoidance of evil and the doing of good (Romans 6: 12).

> "Let not sin therefore reign in your mortal body, that ye should obey it in the lusts thereof."

And even if there are such hypocrites who say: "The new man in us, it is true, does not sin, but indeed the old one," we would like to ask what then has become renewed or has been created anew in them by Christ if the old man is still there?

However, it cannot be avoided that we as real, sanctified children God should be considered pretenders of piety by the children of the world and acclaimed as hypocrites. For the unconverted have no conception of the life in the Spirit and cannot believe that anyone could be in earnest about godliness, inasmuch as they themselves deny the power of the same. But such hypocrites who come in the name of Christ, we shall avoid (II Timothy 3), for they, like actors, merely adopt the costume, script and bearing of another person, falsify themselves into someone else and, besides, are betrayers and mockers of the children of God because, in true godliness, these always and in all places remain what they themselves are, and because of their single-heartedness toward Christ, people think they can do what they please with them. But this is why Christ even recommended to His own that they be not only as harmless as doves but as wise as serpents and guard themselves against the malice of men, as we see this in Christ Himself, in that He proved to the hypocrites that He saw through their mask, and unveiled their wickedness to their own shame (for example Matthew 22 : 15 ff.).

"Then went the Pharisees, and took counsel how they might entangle him in his talk.

"And they sent out unto him their disciples with the Herodians, saying, Master, we know that thou art true, and teachest the way of God in truth, neither carest thou for any man: for thou regardest not the person of men.

"Tell us therefore, What thinkest thou? Is it lawful to give tribute unto Caesar, or not?

"But Jesus perceived their wickedness, and said, Why tempt ye me, ye hypocrites?"

Chapter LXII

The Standard of Truth

January 24, 1841 (Sunday); Afternoon Meeting
I John 3 : 7

"Little children, let no man deceive you: he that doeth righteousness is righteous, even as he is righteous."

John warns the children of light of deception, in reference to the *only* way to blessedness in Christ, namely, the *doing of righteousness,* that they should not let themselves be persuaded about it otherwise by the world, which not only does not know this only way, but even rejects it with scorn and considers it a wrong way of seduction; for in the world one hears warnings of seduction too, but by these it understands exactly the opposite of John's warning which is conversion to faith and to the way of righteousness and of life, through sanctification.

Now, while God's Word warns the children of God of the general wrong way of the world according to which the sinner is pronounced righteous and saved and the children of the devil are declared children of God and heirs of the kingdom; and the world warns of the teaching and the way of the "new" faith and "new" baptists as against the misleading way (because we firmly hold that none by nature are children of God and nothing but children of the devil and that no one can be saved as a sinner but only as a righteous and sanctified man), over and against these warnings, unbelief declares God's Word to be a lie, and asks "If none should be saved except those who do not sin, who then might be saved?" but does not heed Christ's answer (Matthew 19: 26), *With men this is impossible.*

Therefore, they do indeed confess that they are sinful, and sinners, but in doing so are not fair enough to think "If we are sinners, we cannot be of God but are of the devil." In their unrighteousness, they still insist upon being of God and, it is true, God does not hold us accountable for being sinners by nature in Adam, but He wants us to believe Him when He tells us what we do not know about ourselves, that as sinners we are of the devil. However, when the liars say in contradiction, that what the Word of God says is not true, that then is the unpardonable sin of unbelief, and by great contradiction against the Truth, men become hardened and imperceptive so that afterwards nothing can be accomplished for their salvation.

Yet all who let themselves be told what they do not know, because they do not know themselves, and who then acknowledge that God is right and cease to resist (or contradict) Him, soon let it be recognized by them as the Truth and they are saved from the devil's power. It, of course, is hard work until one's natural pride has been broken down so that he is able to recognize himself as a child of the devil (Psalm 14), but there is no rest for the soul otherwise, no way to God, and as soon as one *believes* the Word of God and learns to know himself, he should then become converted and cry to God and so be saved.

But if we know that Christ is the Way and that He is

pure and holy and without sin, it is self-understood that, in Him, we can and shall live without sin. And since this is the only way to God, there is therefore no other seduction for the children of God than that of giving room to the lie,—"that even with sinning one can be saved," and the more subtle this deception is, the more readily it is accepted. Salvation, of course, does not lie in the name alone, namely that one need but to belong to the faction, but in the thing itself, that one live altogether in righteousness. Consequently, for natural men, there is no leading astray because they of themselves already, belong to death and the devil, and their worst deception is that they, in spite of it, with mocking lips, warn against the only way to salvation, that they by no means believe for the sake of being saved!

Zurich, January 26, 1841

With reference to the *sin against the Holy Ghost,* Mark 3 : 28-30 is the clearest passage of what it is ; namely, blasphemy of the Holy Ghost, in any person under the assertion that it is the unclean, *evil spirit of the devil.*

> "Verily I say unto you, All sins shall be forgiven unto the sons of men, and blasphemies wherewith soever they shall blaspheme:
> "But he that shall blaspheme against the Holy Ghost hath never forgiveness, but is in danger of eternal damnation:
> "Because they said, He hath an unclean spirit."

Festus accused Paul of madness and feared . . . . . How much more cause then is there for pronouncing such a sentence against the *wise of this world,* who, for sheer learning, do not find God (I Corinthians 1).

January 26, 1841 (Tuesday) ; Evening Meeting
I John 3 : 7 ff.

"Little children, let no man deceive you: he that doeth righteousness is righteous, even as he is righteous.

"He that committeth sin is of the devil; for the devil sinneth from the beginning. For this purpose the Son of God was manifested, that he might destroy the works of the devil.

"Whosoever is born of God doth not commit sin; for his seed remaineth in him: and he cannot sin, because he is born of God.

"In this the children of God are manifest, and the children of the devil: whosoever doeth not righteousness is not of God, neither he that loveth not his brother."

We have no other standard of the truth than the Word of God for knowing who the children of God and who the children of the devil are, for on that point, the entire Word gives us information about the *true* and the *false*, because the whole world is of the lie. And just as everyone who believes the Truth (the Word of God) soon has a quickening experience of his own and comes to the conviction that God's Word is the Truth and not a lie so that he must affirm, attest and set a seal to the truth of it, so, on the other hand, he who does not believe it, but from the first thinks that what the Word of God says is not true and not possible, never comes to a personal experience with it, but by unbelief cuts himself off from the Living Fountain and makes the fulfilment of the Word impossible for himself because he makes God a liar. For all the promises of God are Yea *in Christ* and Amen *in Him* but not *out of Him*.

Man, of his own effort, may trouble himself about

being righteous as much as he will, he still will not attain the aim and the goal through it. He will merely set up a *human* righteousness according to the old law of the letter and can never attain to *divine* righteousness, which proceeds from the new law of the Spirit and has merit before God only in Christ, for that which is human (one's own) is ever tainted and coupled with sin and therefore is not the righteousness that is acceptable in the sight of God but self-deception and, if one is displaced in it and mistaught, mere hypocrisy.

But the divine righteousness of the children of God (the reborn) of itself is something entire, complete, unadulterated because he who does righteousness cannot *along with it* commit sin inasmuch as the seed of God remains in him who has once, in truth, been begotten and born of God and has become a participant of His divine nature by the communion and indwelling of the Promised Holy Ghost, Who is given to all who receive the Word of Truth in faith. And through the Spirit of sonship perfect love is operative in us, by which we willingly and joyfully fulfil the commandments of God and are no longer governed by the fear of God alone and driven to the good. And the more completely, the more confidingly we remain in God's fellowship, the stronger, the more active and the more blessed we are in doing the will of God, so that the committing of sin is impossible for us because we have become free by the indwelling of divine life and have acquired a thorough disinclination, aversion and horror concerning all the works of darkness.

In regard to sin, the children of God are most severe toward themselves, not toward others like the hypocrites (Matthew 7 : 1).

"Judge not, that ye be not judged."

They are first concerned about the purity and preservation of their own heart and life, so that they preserve great joyousness toward God in the testimony of a good conscience, and only in this way can they work for others with real success. In this respect, we shall observe carefully how John describes both the children of God and the children of the devil, so that we are not mistaken or deceived about ourselves or others. He characterizes both from two sides, affirmatively and privatively (positively and negatively).

The affirmative side of the children of God is: *They do righteousness* and love the brethren; the privative side: They do not commit sin because they are born of God and the seed of the Father (the Spirit of the Son) abides in them as their eternal light and life and power of sanctification, through and through, according to spirit and soul and body (I Thessalonians 5:23) to preserve them blameless until the end, until the coming of Christ.

> "And the very God of peace sanctify you wholly; and I pray God your whole spirit and soul and body be preserved blameless unto the coming of our Lord Jesus Christ."

The affirmative side of the children of the devil is: They commit sin; the privative: *They do not do righteousness* and do not love the brethren.

However, the *positive* side of each of the two is so strongly preponderant and predominant that the negative side of itself—and necessarily—follows for that reason, so that everyone who does the righteousness of God does not, with it, commit sin (because sin is of the devil and the devil no longer has any power in the children of God inasmuch as Christ in them has destroyed the works of the devil). But everyone who still commits sin does not, with it, do the righteousness of God (because God's seed does not dwell in him but the devil's).

The mystery therefore lies in the acceptance of the *Word of God* as the Truth, and although it punishes and condemns us in the beginning, yet, afterwards, it renews, quickens and saves us by setting the seal of the Holy Ghost upon us.

CHAPTER LXIII

THE TWO WAYS

January 28, 1841 (Thursday); Evening Meeting
I John 3:7 ff.

"Little children, let no man deceive you," or delude you, mislead you by the judgment of the world in reference to the difference between the children of God and the children of the devil and concerning the two ways to salvation and condemnation, for therein have all men been deceived. Among all those who are the devil's, there is not a single one who would consider himself a child of his, for all assume the right of sonship to God, and by that very thing make the Word of God a lie, which so definitely declares that everyone who does not do righteousness but commits sin is not of God but of the devil and that, as a consequence, the whole world lies in wickedness and is full of the children of the devil.

Concerning this testimony of the truth, Christ came upon the cross (Matthew 23; John 7:7; 8:44) and on account of it all servants of God have suffered the hatred of the world, persecution, and death.

> "The world cannot hate you; but me it hateth, because I testify of it, that the works thereof are evil."

> "Ye are of your father the devil, and the lusts of your father ye will do. He was a murderer from the beginning, and abode not in the truth, because there is no truth in him. When he speaketh a lie, he speaketh of his own: for he is a liar, and the father of it."

For how will anyone be converted to God from the power of Satan if he does not believe the Word of God, that all men by nature — without exception — are sinners and children of the devil? And how can anyone be saved without conversion (Acts 26:18; I Thessalonians 1:9)?

> "To open their eyes, and to turn them from darkness to light, and from the power of Satan unto God, that they may receive forgiveness of sins, and inheritance among them which are sanctified by faith that is in me."

> "For they themselves shew of us what manner of entering in we had unto you, and how ye turned to God from idols to serve the living and true God;"

But when one really acknowledges God's right in this, he becomes converted, saved, and the veil is removed from his eyes, that he must perceive the truth and confess that heretofore he, like all the others, was a child of wrath and of the devil and *only in Christ* did he receive the power to become a child of God. Therefore we should observe well the sharp, striking contrast John makes between the children of God and the children of the devil so that we may not deceive ourselves in this most important thing of all; for if a man considers himself a son of God and nevertheless is not one but one of the devil, who but himself suffers the loss? But if we behold ourselves in this clear mirror of the Word, where we stand will indeed be revealed to us, for when the apostle says: "He that doeth righteousness is righteous; he that committeth sin is of the devil," we learn from it, that to be righteous and to be a child of God is one and the same thing and that to be a sinner and a child of the devil is the same.

And according to that description, the children of God in the world are few but the children of the devil, many. Proud sinners may strive against this conclusion as much as they like, the Word of God still is and remains true against the lie of those who are of the devil and make themselves children of God and dare, besides, to say of His Word, "It is not true!" without considering that this lie is their greatest sin, more grievous than thievery, adultery and murder for these sins can be forgiven but the other sin cannot be. Now if we should ask whether there are few who are saved, Jesus does not say whether there are many or few in Luke 13:23 and 24 but "Strive to enter in at the strait gate."

> "Then said one unto him, Lord, are there few that be saved? And he said unto them,
> "Strive to enter in at the strait gate: for many, I say unto you, will seek to enter in, and shall not be able."

Therefore whoever finds that he is not yet fashioned in Christ as the Word of God requires, shall have to strive further in all earnestness that he may be.

January 31, 1841 (Sunday); Morning Meeting
I John 3:7 ff.

> "Little children, let no man deceive you: he that doeth righteousness is righteous, even as he is righteous.

> "He that committeth sin is of the devil; for the devil sinneth from the beginning. For this purpose the Son of God was manifested, that he might destroy the works of the devil.
>
> "Whosoever is born of God doth not commit sin; for his seed remaineth in him: and he cannot sin, because he is born of God.
>
> "In this the children of God are manifest, and the children of the devil: whosoever doeth not righteousness is not of God, neither he that loveth not his brother."

The apostle teaches us two things here: (a) what the way to life and to condemnation is (Matthew 25:46)

> "And these shall go away into everlasting punishment: but the righteous into life eternal."

and (b) who the children of God and the children of the devil are, i.e., who may be saved here and who may not. The world is in error concerning both. For they will not be children of the devil, and will yet be *saved as sinners* because Christ died for sin. But Christ has not died for sin so as to leave us in it, that we could continue in sin and still be children of God, but rather to redeem us from sin so that we may not continue to be children of the devil (Romans 6).

For in the death of Christ there lies not only the *forgiveness of sin* that it may nevermore be punished, as the false believers interpret it (for sin is ever punishable before God), but Christ died for this purpose, that He might extirpate, abolish, put an end to, destroy *sin itself* as the devil's realm and work in man so that we may *sin no more*. For if sinners as such could be saved, Christ would not have come into the world to die for them and to make an end to sinning, and in that way a great amount of darkness would come into the fellowship of God, which is not agreeable to His nature and combinable with His holy being.

Yet the world understands nothing else by the death and reconciliation of Christ than this, that, by the same, the privilege of salvation was given to sinners and no one thinks that this, to begin with and strictly speaking, has reference to the dying of the old man and the awakening of the new one in us. But because the mystery of faith lies in just this, it is also evident that the doing of righteousness is just as natural and innate for a man of God as the committing of sin is for one of the devil. Now, as it is the devil in the latter who produces sin by his seed, so it is Christ in the former Who works righteousness.

The divine seed of regeneration is not transmitted to children by natural generation, as sin is in Adam, but a new birth from above is still required for children of believing parents and therefore holy parents should rear their children in the Word of God (Ephesians 6:4).

> "And, ye fathers, provoke not your children to wrath: but bring them up in the nurture and admonition of the Lord."

And yet, even so, there lies in the seed of God a propagative power that germinates in others, be it by word or simply by a holy life (I Peter 3:1)

> "Likewise, ye wives, be in subjection to your own husbands; that, if any obey not the word, they also may without the word be won by the conversation of the wives;"

and if in this respect the believers do not deserve their name, they give offense to the Gospel.

But because it is the devil in man who commits sin, he must be separated from man, or man must be rescued from him through Christ's death (Romans 7); and because it even so is Christ in man Who does the righteousness, one cannot ascribe it to man and it should therefore not be declared as impossible either because sin is not more in keeping with man than righteousness, but the opposite. The working of righteousness does, of course, not belong to fallen man of himself, except, perhaps, only in single instances of human and civic righteousness and it happens so seldom that when something of the kind does come to light, it is looked upon as a wonder and is trumpeted forth and published in the annals of noble deeds. Yet truly divine righteousness finds no such recognition but rather contradiction, for children of God testify of that which they have experienced of the Word of Life within them; namely, that no natural and no unconverted man is of God, or works the righteousness of God; neither can he be saved. Therefore all the natural ones are condemned, which the world in its self-love and self-righteousness will never admit, and consequently decries the children of God as slanderers—as those who like to condemn—and hates and persecutes them; although it is not their pleasure to judge others without mercy but God's truth.

January 31, 1841 (Sunday); Afternoon Meeting
I John 3:9 ff.

"Whosoever is born of God doth not commit sin; for his seed remaineth in him: and he cannot sin, because he is born of God.

"In this the children of God are manifest, and the children of the devil: whosoever doeth not righteousness is not of God, neither he that loveth not his brother.

"For this is the message that ye heard from the beginning, that we should love one another.

"Not as Cain, who was of that wicked one, and slew his brother. And wherefore slew he him? Because his own works were evil, and his brother's righteous."

John makes a supposition: "Whosoever is born of God" and from it draws the conclusion: "doth not commit sin." We shall therefore know who is born of God or what it means to be born of God. In general, a child of God is the exact opposite of the natural man, and one first becomes a child of God through a new birth and creation of God in Christ, so that Christ, after the manner of His Spirit, will dwell in the heart of man as the *seed of God* and only in Him can we see and learn *what* a child of God is and *why* each one in whom Christ lives does not sin.

Many deceive themselves in this: they place or seek the sonship of God in something in which it does not subsist, and with their fancied faith continue in sin because they are not truly converted and reborn and their heart is not cleansed from the roots of the old man. They seek not single-heartedly, nor are they minded for that which is above but for that which is on earth, and therefore the requirement of a sinless life is declared to be extravagant and impossible, in that they do with the Gospel what the Pharisees of Old did with the law, who omitted the hardest and most important parts and satisfied themselves with the miserable patchwork of human righteousness. Thus also would the same hypocrites willingly accept

Christ as the Reconciler of Sin but not as the Life from the Father.

But no one can be a half-Christian, that he should bear the name of Christ and still do the works of the devil. Neither has Christ come and died for the righteous but for the ungodly and sinners who in their natural perdition recognize and confess themselves to be children of the devil, in order that they might be healed by Christ the Physician, and inasmuch as all without distinction are equal sinners in Adam (also the apparently good and pious) and as one only in Christ receives the power of sonship of God, no one is or becomes a child of God without conversion, renewal and rebirth through the Holy Spirit. In all who are born of God there dwells the one and same Spirit of Christ, in which all are like-minded and know, understand and love one another. But where the spirit of the world still dwells, there things are not in keeping with the Spirit of God, and the two kinds of men are opposed and contrary to each other according to their nature, as were Cain and Abel.

The devil may represent himself as pious as he will in his children, just as Cain, for appearance's sake, also wished to bring a sacrifice, like Abel, and yet he was from the wicked one and hated his righteous brother. Abel's sacrifice was the expression of a humble, contrite heart in a feeling of human misery, of simplicity, of nothingness and sin, whereas conceited Cain thought that he had brought something to God by his sacrifice and was also deserving. A child of God never thinks of bringing a sacrifice to God in this self-righteous spirit and considers it grace that he can do the will of God, and when he has done all that was asked of him, he still feels that he is an unprofitable servant and does not think that he has done anything.

Now, as the natural man is a sinner and not a child of God, so is the reborn one a righteous man and not a sinner or child of the devil, and this stamps itself upon his entire life as a firm and stedfast character that may not be shaken by outer circumstances or by the temptations of the devil and his children. It is also absurd that Christ is said to dwell or lie dormant as an embryo or seed in every person born, so that He needs only to be awakened and that, accordingly, all would be saved in the course of time (as certain people say); whereas more correctly speaking it is the seed of the devil—sin and death—that dwells in every person born which must first be uprooted and removed before Christ can dwell and be fashioned in man.

February 2, 1841 (Tuesday); Evening Meeting
I John 3:8 ff.

> "He that committeth sin is of the devil; for the devil sinneth from the beginning. For this purpose the Son of God was manifested, that he might destroy the works of the devil.
>
> "Whosoever is born of God doth not commit sin; for his seed remaineth in him: and he cannot sin, because he is born of God.
>
> "In this the children of God are manifest, and the children of the devil: whosoever doeth not righteousness is not of God, neither he that loveth not his brother."

John speaks in antitheses:

> "He that committeth sin is of the devil;
> "Whosoever is born of God doth not commit sin;
> "Whosoever doeth not righteousness is not of God."

That is, every tree bears the fruit that it is possible for it to bear according to its kind and nature, and by the fruit the tree is known (Matthew 12:33).

> "Either make the tree good, and his fruit good; or else make the tree corrupt, and his fruit corrupt: for the tree is known by his fruit."

Thus, in regard to the fruit, all things come about naturally and in this one can force or affect nothing. It depends entirely upon the spirit that is in man, whether it is the spirit of the world or the Spirit of God, and that which comes forth from one is still according to it—be it good or evil, bitter or sweet—and there is no mixture of the two kinds of spirits: one is, rightly, only of God or of the devil, does righteousness or sin in his every-day life according to his own kind, nature and habit.

A child of God, always and everywhere, in private as in public life, presents himself the same—without pretense. He has no special *times, days, hours* when he would like to be holier than he is otherwise, as the hypocrites of the world perhaps restrain themselves from their usual diversions on special occasions (high feast days) and for this reason consider the children of God, in whom godliness in its power is something habitual and constant, low-spirited people, hypocritical devotees, etc., because they are aware of their origin of God and of His dwelling in them and never deny their divine origin. On the whole, they do not live otherwise than is their way.

Christ does not give His Spirit to anyone unless he has been purified beforehand of the old ways of the flesh, or of the spirit of the world. The cask must not only be emptied of the old wine (by the forgiveness of sin) but of the dregs as well, by purification from the indwelling sin of the old nature of the devil and here, then, the Holy Spirit in man is a new spirit indeed (John 7:39) which one has not had or known before,

> "(But this spake he of the Spirit, which they that believe on him should receive: for the Holy Ghost was not yet given; because that Jesus was not yet glorified.)"

and from this Living Fountain a *new life* flows of itself and inevitably, so that it would be impossible for the children of God to fall easily in gross sins because it would be offensive to their nature. In fact, it is incomprehensible to them that a child of the devil (against his nature) at times does something that is good and righteous too. However, these things are not only rare exceptions to the rule according to which they live, but if looked at rightly they are not truly good (in God's sight), but one's own self-gratification does not, on that account, stop him from being a child of the devil, whose spirit is nevertheless in him.

Likewise, it seems that a child of God sometimes does something wrong and sinful too, if in an unguarded moment he is surprised and overtaken in a fault, contrary to Jesus' manner, nature and custom. But he is immediately punished, disciplined and grieved in the Spirit, so that he needs no further outward punishment but rather some encouragement (Galatians 6:1),

> "Brethren, if a man be overtaken in a fault, ye which are spiritual, restore such an one in the spirit of meekness; considering thyself, lest thou also be tempted."

neither does he, by this, exactly fall from his state of grace of the sonship of God, although he should guard and keep himself from such overhastiness also. One can,

of course, fall from grace back into sin by continual unfaithfulness. Therefore we need but to take note of which
spirit dwells and reigns in one, what kind of way and
nature he manifests in his ordinary every-day life, to
know whether he is of God or of the devil.

Chapter LXIV

"Keep Thy Heart With All Diligence"

February 4, 1841 (Thursday); Evening Meeting
I John 3 : 9

We must observe how John understood the expressions,
"to commit sin" and "to do righteousness," in order that
we may not comprehend them otherwise. Each of these
expressions indicates the inborn nature and inner state
of the heart of man, be that as it may, of God or of the
devil. Thus everyone must manifest himself as he is and
he cannot deny his nature, and as the doing of sin is inseparable from the children of the devil, so is the doing
of righteousness inseparable from the children of God.
Both are based upon an inner necessity, as a result of
which a good tree cannot do otherwise than bring forth
good fruit, and as soon as one takes the latter away, whatever remains of a good tree falls away also; i.e., whoever
does not live in righteousness (as in the divine nature)
is for that reason not a child of God.

But just because the doing of righteousness is necessary in a child of God, he ascribes his justification and
acceptableness before God not to the doing of a single
good work but to his blessed rebirth and sonship of God,
which must already exist before the good work and
from which the good works must needs come forth. The

merit of his works lies not in themselves but in the faith and mind of the Spirit, from which they proceed. Good works are the outward proof that he himself is good. And so it is reversed with evil works also, which necessarily proceed from the evil foundation of the heart for what one says or does, comes forth from one's heart (Matthew 12:34 ff.; 15:13), be it good or evil.

"O generation of vipers, how can ye, being evil, speak good things? for out of the abundance of the heart the mouth speaketh.

"A good man out of the good treasure of the heart bringeth forth good things: and an evil man out of the evil treasure bringeth forth evil things.

"But I say unto you, That every idle word that men shall speak, they shall give account thereof in the day of judgment.

"For by thy words thou shalt be justified, and by thy words thou shalt be condemned."

"But he answered and said, Every plant, which my heavenly Father hath not planted, shall be rooted up."

A child of God in whom God's seed remains, can then bring forth no evil because God (the Only One Who is good) dwells in him and not the devil (the evil one), and no sin, nothing evil comes forth from God (James 1:13)

"Let no man say when he is tempted, I am tempted of God: for God cannot be tempted with evil, neither tempteth he any man:"

but always from the devil, and because the devil no longer dwells in the children of God, anything evil can make itself felt in the heart only by temptation. However, if it is not harbored—nourished—but is instantly suppressed at its very beginning, as soon as the Spirit testifies: "Be careful, that is not from the Father but from the world; the serpent lies hidden there!" a secret, sinful impulse cannot become a deed. For all the evil that one does must first have risen up in the heart and have been nourished (unless one were suddenly and unexpectedly provoked to it), and then if it is a sin unto death one dies because of it.

Therefore, the rule of the children of God is "Keep thy heart with all diligence; for out of it are the issues of life (Proverbs 4:23)." The great difference lies herein: in God's work in man and in the work produced according to the law. For when one is awakened from the sleep of sin, he, of himself, desires to do righteousness and so builds God a temple, with his own hands, to be worshipped in, as did Solomon; but when Christ comes and breaks through with His real joys of life, this temple of the law is then so completely demolished that not one stone is left upon another, and in its place Christ builds a new temple of the Spirit, in the heart of man, in which God resides, reveals His glory, and is worshipped in spirit and in truth for merchants, thieves and murderers reside in the temple of the law as they always have done heretofore.

February 7, 1841 (Sunday); Morning Meeting
I John 3:8 ff.

"He that committeth sin is of the devil;"

———————

"Whosoever is born of God doth not commit sin;"

It would be as impossible as it would be useless to

enumerate in detail what is sin. He who has not himself known sin would not be helped, but he who has recognized it through divine enlightenment knows that all is sin that militates against divine purity, holiness, righteousness and truth and that all sin is of the devil and not of God. And as sin is, so also is the sinner himself, as long as he remains in sin and is not reconciled to God through Christ.

But as soon as one is awakened by Christ to observe himself in relation to God, so soon does sin and the knowledge of it become the first and most important thing with him, for he learns to understand that he as a sinner is not of God and, as such, cannot come to God, and as he learns to know sin, he takes delight in God's law in relation to the inner man and begins to cleanse himself after the manner of the law. But he soons finds that the law of sin in his members strives against him and takes him captive so that he cannot do the good he longs to do (Romans 7). Then Christ as the Way, the Truth and the Life becomes necessary as the *Mediator* between God and man, so that the impossible may become possible. Therefore through Christ we must descend from God and be born anew according to the Spirit, so as to go, through the Son, to the Father as His children because the Son has appeared for the purpose of effecting this great change in us.

The expressions, "to be of the devil" and "to be of God," therefore refer to the spirit which dwells and reigns in man, in that the spirit of man takes on either the way and nature of God or that of the devil (light or darkness); indeed according to whether the Spirit of God or the spirit of the world rules in him, for according to the body we are always *creatures of God,* but according to the spirit, the sinners are not of God but of the devil, and the righteous are not of the devil but of God and, indeed, no longer merely creatures of God (in Christ) but His own begotten children, and if the Spirit of God governs us, the doing of righteousness comes forth of itself.

By this sign of the Spirit in man the children of God are to be known and distinguished from the children of the devil, even though the latter falsely apply to themselves the word of the apostle: "Whoever is born of God doth not commit sin; . . . and he cannot sin," and say, "We have been born of God and therefore we sin no more." And all the while they wallow in the lusts of the flesh they insist that this concerns only their flesh and not their spirit. But if the spirit has been liberated for righteousness, the flesh can no longer serve sin but must follow the spirit in the service of righteousness (Romans 6). Against such lying, one must rather say: "Whosoever has been born of God does not commit sin; therefore you are not of God but of the wicked one, whose work and will you do."

Now, John does not say this for the purpose of judging others, those who sin, but so that each one should apply it to himself. "He that committeth sin is of the devil." It is shocking that *by their committing sin* the devil drives men so far that they *destroy themselves,* which would be unthinkable if sin were not a spirit of madness. The world does not know God, but His *children* shall so represent Him and His nature that, through them, men may learn to know Him even as through the Son Himself.

February 7, 1841 (Sunday); Afternoon Meeting
I John 3:9

"Whosoever is born of God doth not commit sin; for his seed remaineth in him: and he cannot sin, because he is born of God."

From the foregoing, we shall have convinced ourselves that there are two kinds of people: children of God and children of the devil, and according to the description there are more of the latter than of the former. He who does not do righteousness is not of God and is therefore of the devil, whose will he does, and through the disposition of the flesh he is an enemy of God and is also his own enemy; for as much as one sinner can harm another, he still harms himself most, in that he commits sin, and as long as sin dwells in man and he lives in it, so long has the devil his power, claim and right upon him and can say, "This is my property (comes from me)." And as long as the devil has his own work in man, man is not *free*, is no child of God, because he is not in Christ but in *Adam*, whose death we have inherited and bear in us and for which Christ died, that He might abolish this first death, take it away from us, and in its place give us His eternal life, for in that Christ died He died unto sin, i.e., for us and the whole world. Therefore if sin still dwells in us and we live in it, it indeed is not dead and we have not died with Christ and consequently it is as if Christ had not died for us.

Therefore each one must be converted to Christ and give back to the devil that which belongs to him, so that he may no longer have or make any claim on us on behalf of sin, just as he had none on and in Christ, and if it does not come thus far with us, we have not put Christ on or taken the old man off. But he who does not *here* come out of the first death in Adam, falls into the second death afterwards because he has not accepted the *salvation in Christ*.

For we all indeed bear the first death in us by nature

since no one is born otherwise, but as we have put it on in Adam, so ought we to let it be put off in Christ and, in return, receive life from God in the Son. Inasmuch as John says (verse 14): "We know that we have passed from death unto life, because we love the brethren," he acknowledges and confesses that all pardoned children of God were beforetime in death also, and the transition takes place only by faith in the Gospel and baptism in Christ, by which we are freed from the devil, and in Christ enter not only into a new relationship to God as His children, but also to one another as brothers and sisters, upon which our holy brotherly love is established. But if we have not put off the old man and each one would bring the old villain and devil with him, there would be no brotherly love and no fellowship of saints even in spite of baptism.

But where faith has grasped the mystery of the death of Christ, there baptism certainly attains its purpose of planting one together with Christ into the likeness of His death and resurrection. Here ends the excuse that it is impossible because Christ lets all be told, "Come, for all things are ready!" And if in Adam the first death and the power of the devil were so great that all have died on that account, how much more in Christ must life become mighty over death so as to make void all claims of the devil upon the children of God! But unbelief and disobedience with respect to the Gospel robs men of their salvation, as was the case with the Jews (Hebrews 5:9).

> "And being made perfect, he became the author of eternal salvation unto all them that obey him;"

However, the passing over from death to life does not take place without our knowing about it and the excuse of the impossibility of it is the worst lie of the devil against the Word of God. A child of God is not indifferent in his thinking so that he would do nothing about it if some sin should still be found; instead he purifies himself of all sin so as to please God.

Chapter LXV

The Hidden Reason for the Believers' Endurance

February 9, 1841 (Tuesday); Evening Meeting
I John 3:10

> "In this the children of God are manifest, and the children of the devil: whosoever doeth not righteousness is not of God, neither he that loveth not his brother."

John sums up the essence of the children of God in these two characteristics: do righteousness and love the brethren. With the children of the devil it is the opposite: commit sin and hate mankind. In what relation the two stand to each other, John points out by the examples of the first two men born, Cain and Abel, who as children of Adam were of course both sinners, but yet there was a difference in their minds and dispositions: Cain bold, defiant, surrendered and sold to sin with the desire to practise it, without offering the least resistance (Genesis 4:6);

> "And the Lord said unto Cain, Why art thou wroth? and why is thy countenance fallen?"

but Abel, of a humble, contrite heart on account of the fall and its sad consequences troubled himself about resisting sin. His works were *righteous* but Cain's were wicked and for that reason Cain hated his brother and slew him, so that hatred is the crown of all evil works, the utmost, the last, most atrocious thing to which a person does not come unless he has given himself up to sin entirely.

Thus there is still a difference among sinners, always according to whether one lives in a God-fearing or in an ungodly manner. But this difference occurs only under the law, which condemns only the unnatural deed-sins but not the disposition of the heart (as the catechism signifies). As God knows that the thoughts and endeavors of man are evil already from his youth (Genesis 8:21),

> "And the Lord smelled a sweet savour; and the Lord said in his heart, I will not again curse the ground any more for man's sake; for the imagination of man's heart is evil from his youth; neither will I again smite any more every thing living, as I have done."

He therefore imputes natural, inborn, indwelling sin to no one to condemnation, for Christ has died on that account. But man should guard himself from unnatural sin, which is already recognized and punished by the law of nature, inasmuch as no human society could exist otherwise, for men would tear one another to pieces like wild animals tear their prey apart, if they had not to fear the punishment of unnatural sins. But it is not necessary for man to commit unnatural sins against the law, for which even the heathen have no excuse and which they can avoid, without having any glory or righteousness before God for that reason; and if one appears righteous in this respect before men, he is so only in comparison to others.

Thus was Abel righteous as compared to Cain, because

he feared God and shunned sin. But, as for himself, Abel was still a sinner, yet his inborn sin was covered and forgiven by Christ's sacrifice. But under the New Testament (in Christ), the new law of the Spirit (love) is implanted in the believers and saints (children of God) instead of the old law of the letter; and the new law does not extend itself so far as to come up to the outward deeds of sin, but only to the disposition of the heart, which God alone sees and regards, whereas men regard, judge and punish only the outward deed.

According to this new standard, only he is righteous before God whose heart has been purified from indwelling sin, out of which then—inevitably—a holy life flows; and as only unnatural deed-sins were forbidden and condemned under the old law, so, according to the new law, natural sins and the disposition of the flesh (which is enmity toward God) are already forbidden and condemned, for no one is in Christ except him in whom sin has been abolished. Therefore Christ (Matthew 5) says, "Ye have heard that it was said by them of old, Thou shalt not kill; Thou shalt not commit adultery, . . . But I say unto you, . . ."

Christ judges the thoughts of the heart, not only the outward works, and for that reason John says, "Whosoever hateth his brother is a murderer:" for every murder must first be present in the heart (in the disposition) and before God that counts as much as the deed itself according to the new law, which demands a clean heart.

February 11, 1841 (Thursday); Evening Meeting
I John 3:11

> "For this is the message that ye heard from
> the beginning, that we should love one an-
> other."

The apostle says this only to the children of God, whose nature has become divine love because they are of God Who is Love, as hatred is the manner and nature of the devil and his children, and because the latter cannot love, one cannot command them to love, for love has no law but is itself a law for the children of God, whom one, by all means, can bid to love, if they will not deny their nature and descent from God and become like the children of the devil, for one cannot have the devil's work and drive in one's self without being his child. Therefore the children of God permit no motive in them that they know is not of God but of the devil, and to it all say "Be gone!"

For God leads us into possession of the Promised Land (of the heart), only on the condition that we unsparingly destroy all the old inhabitants (sin), without letting any remain (like Israel in Canaan), lest they become a snare and pitfall to us, quell us again, and as a result we ourselves would be cast out of the Promised Land (like Israel). Now, whoever loves sin and stands in league with it, cannot love himself for his salvation's sake, but hates himself, is his own enemy, and will be lost eternally because sin is the destruction of man. God Himself, in that He so loved the ungodly, sinful world that He gave His Only Begotten Son for it, by that revealed His hatred of sin, so as to destroy it and save us from it, if we *will* be saved, so that we no longer remain sinners and are lost but become children of God and are saved.

Thus we must, as children of God, also have the mind of the Father, love what He loves (namely the souls of men unto the salvation of the same) and hate what He hates (namely sin in man). True love of God is zealous and wages war against sin, but men are so senselessly in love with sin that they will not let themselves be punished by, or separated from, it and hate Christ and His witnesses of the truth, persecuting them even unto death. Therefore no one who has become a believer can love his soul and save it unto eternal life unless he hates his life in this world, for if we love our own life, we apostatize in temptation, deny Christ, and lose our salvation. This false love of one's self is the *most subtle sin,* the hidden snare by which the devil catches the believers who will not be an offscouring, an expiatory sacrifice, and a spectacle in the world for Christ's sake but would still like to be *something* here.

Indeed, in no other way than by loving his own life in this world can a believer be overcome again, for in doing so he loves sin to his own ruination. But he who hates his life, namely that it is all the same to him what the world does with him, attains the goal of salvation (Luke 12; Romans 14:7).

> "For none of us liveth to himself, and no
> man dieth to himself."

Herein lies the hidden reason why not all believers endure until the end so as to be saved (Matthew 13), namely, in the love of their own life, and Paul therefore says to them (II Corinthians 11:2 f.):

> "For I am jealous over you with godly
> jealousy: ...
> "But I fear, lest by any means, as the serpent beguiled Eve through his subtilty, so your minds should be corrupted from the simplicity that is in Christ."

Oh, it is unbelievable how the serpent twines himself around in man and yet knows how to slink away so as not to make sin apparent! Besides, the devil does not hate the children of God without a reason. He knows very well why he oppresses them and certainly that on account of which we are reviled and persecuted, is exactly what we should preserve and in which our strength and salvation lies. It is that very treasure which God has given us, and Christ is so exceedingly great that we are not worthy even to suffer for Him, much less that we should be ashamed or afraid.

February 14, 1841 (Sunday) ; Morning Meeting
I John 3 : 11

> "For this is the message that ye heard from the beginning, that we should love one another."

The children of God must learn love from their Father, just as the children of the devil have received hatred from their father, that they hate the good and the souls of men but love the evil. But God loves mankind and hates the evil—sin—and has condemned it in Christ in order that it would be separated from us and killed in us as the old man with all his inclinations and motives, as the law in our members that resists not only the law of God but also the law of the better mind in the awakened man, because it is the law of the world and enmity against God or is from the devil, which must be abolished through the death of Christ when man lets himself be reconciled with God (Romans 8 : 2 ; II Corinthians 5).

> "For the law of the Spirit of life in Christ Jesus hath made me free from the law of sin and death."

Where the law of the Spirit of Life in Christ appears, there the law of sin and death in one's members ends, so that the man of God no longer may be a debtor to walk after the flesh, but after the spirit. To a child of God, Christ is his life and therefore his heart and mind and walk is drawn away from the earth and is in heaven, where his treasure is in good security, where thieves cannot steal it as they can man's treasure on earth. For if a believer is not free or loosed in his spirit from the visible, but divided and bound, the devil lays hold of him with his temptations on this very side of the visible, for as long as we are in the world we are exposed to the attacks of the devil and the world and we must be tried and become approved here, whether our faith is an idle word and knowledge or an overcoming power of God through the love of God (Romans 8:35).

> "Who shall separate us from the love of Christ? shall tribulation, or distress, or persecution, or famine, or nakedness, or peril, or sword?"

Therefore, Christ, above all, demands self-denial in every follower (Matthew 16:24),

> "Then said Jesus unto his disciples, If any man will come after me, let him deny himself, and take up his cross, and follow me."

that we, accordingly, hate our life in this world and in the fire-test and melting-pot our faith may become manifest, whether it is gold, silver, precious stones or resin-, hay- and stubble-work that perishes in the fire (I Corinthians 3) for the real purgatory of the children of God is in this world.

Where the work of a teacher must be made known, there the believers are accounted as sheep for the slaughter, and he who would not willingly let himself be laid upon the slaughter-bench as Christ was for us, is not immovably rooted in Him through love so as to bear fruit and keep the faith, but will apostatize in temptation and deny Christ and, out of love for the earthly and for his own life, forfeit the eternal and veritable, like Esau who forfeited his birthright for a morsel of meat.

We cannot love Christ as our real and eternal life if we love our life in this world, for one contradicts the other: where Christ shall live, there man must die; but where one will live for himself, there Christ must die. It is for this reason that three-fourths of those who have heard and have partly believed the Word of God come to shame, for the love of the earthly and visible is so deeply rooted in man that only few allow themselves to be freed from it. Yes, Christ says that it would be impossible for man to enter into the kingdom of God by himself: if God did not make it possible, no one would be saved. Much is required before one merely comes to the beginning of faith, to acknowledge why Christ died, but how much more will be to attain to the *approved* faith that nothing is able or in a position to separate from the love of God, because on the proving ground the love of the earthly suffuses the love to Christ.

February 14, 1841 (Sunday); Afternoon Meeting
I John 3 : 11

> "For this is the message ..., that we should love one another."

John does not say "command" but "message" (and a good message indeed), over which everyone should rightly rejoice, that, through Christ, love instead of hate should again be among men because He destroys the works of the devil, by which he has ruined and sundered all (Titus 3 : 3).

"For we ourselves also were sometimes foolish, disobedient, deceived, serving divers lusts and pleasures, living in malice and envy, hateful, and hating one another."

Of course, it is not yet accomplished in that it is proclaimed to men and for that reason they cannot yet love one another. But the message of peace should nevertheless make them realize that the hatred of men toward one another is of the devil and not befitting of men. And as many as are able to know what belongs to their peace, receive the *love* of God in place of the devilish ill will by which they must reciprocally destroy and ruin one another and, indeed, not according to the will of God (I Timothy 2), but because the devil has his pleasure in setting men at enmity with God and with one another, so as to lead them to condemnation.

Therefore, in His mercy, God offers love and peace to men in Jesus Christ and does not impute their natural sins to them but summons them to reconciliation, and only those are condemned who, in spite of it, persist in their enmity and the disposition of the flesh. If men know their designation of God and were adequate to it, they, as such, would *now already h*ave to recognize and love one another among themselves as "brethren." But by nature that is not the case. Instead, just as they are unjust in their relationship to God, so are they unjust toward one another—proud, lustful of power, hateful, contemptible, embittering life one for the other by sin— and do not even know that that is of the devil in whose power they are.

Therefore, all reasonable men should withdraw themselves from this unjust lordship of the devil and become converted to Christ Who, instead of enmity and hatred, brings us peace and love to save us here and yonder. And for that reason we also should recognize it as a good message, that He lets it be proclaimed to us, in order that in Him we may be translated into the right relationship of children of God and of brethren and members of one body in Christ, who are filled with one Spirit and ruled by one Spirit—Christ—and indeed by holy baptism (I Corinthians 12), when faith has laid hold of and apprehended the Gospel. This cannot possibly be attained by the baptism of infants because in later life, in spite of it, men do not love, but hate, one another and make carnal discriminations, which is not so in the body of Christ (in the church of the saints) ; nor can it be for in all true believers the spirit of the world has been driven out and through the Spirit of Christ all are one.

For One is Master here, not many, and all are brethren in Christ and equal to one another, and he who wishes to be the greatest here shall be the least and the servant of all, that each one, by humility of heart, consider himself the least, just as the Savior has come, not to let Himself be served but to serve and to give His life as a ransom for many. Therefore all are one heart and one soul in Christ because the same Spirit of Christ is in all. However, where love is not found among the believers, there all else is and counts as nothing (I Corinthians 13) ; but meekness is the source of love just as high-mindedness is the source of hatred.

I still conducted a special meeting of the members in the evening from six to nine o'clock for the admonition of all, on account of the great indifference and coldness of most of them.

Chapter LXVI

Holy Brotherly Love, The Treasure of the Children of God

February 16, 1841 (Tuesday) ; Evening Meeting
I John 3 : 11

We should love one another and indeed not with only a common love because publicans and heathen can also love one another (Matthew 5 : 43),

> "Ye have heard that it hath been said, Thou shalt love thy neighbor, and hate thine enemy."

and in doing so still live in hatred, but with a holy, inviolable love in Christ, which, as such, is something entirely new—a fellowship of the saints, a bond of perfection— which unites the children of God as brethren in Jesus Christ and members of His holy body, the church; into which we must enter here, *on earth,* by true conversion and rebirth, and through which we enter into the inseparable union and spiritual relationship with all the saints who have been from all time and whom we do not yet know, until their manifestation with Christ. But a desire and longing to learn to know them all should live in us because God makes His manifold wisdom known to His church by unfolding His wonders of grace in guiding every single one, "which things [even] the angels desire to look into (I Peter 1 ; Ephesians 3 : 10)."

> "To the intent that now unto the principalities and powers in heavenly places might be known by the church the manifold wisdom of God,"

The little we learn about these things here should urge us on to learn to know the great whole, in eternity. For *now* we see in part, and darkly, but *then* from face to face, and herein will the blessedness of the perfected righteous consist, that they will know the wonders of God in His elect and saints and will be known as a part of the whole. For every redeemed one is a wonder of God because God's ways with His children are not our own ways and we ourselves would not have so chosen things.

Upon this foundation true brotherly love and fellowship of the saints now rests, so that all may be sanctified in Christ by the new creation, because love is not from men but from God, for which reason also it is not to be found with men but only with the children of God. For the true fellowship of Christ is still hidden, and what one in this world calls the Christian church is not at all the church of Christ, but the devil has thus imitated it to deceive men, lest they should become converted from darkness to light, and instead of being saints the false Christians carry on their mockery of them. Therefore we may not continue to remain in this false church if we wish to belong to the community of the saints, but must go out therefrom by a real conversion from the power of Satan to God.

Those, really, are not true believers and children of God who, as far as they themselves are concerned, wish to remain alone and have no desire for fellowship; consequently have no brotherly love either, for they are sick. For the blessedness of the children of God subsists in their fellowship, that they may reciprocally communicate with one another for their edification in the love of the brethren. This holy brotherly love is the treasure of the children of God, of which they would not let themselves be robbed at any price and for which they are zealous that it may not be destroyed by the cunning of the devil.

And yet, even where a child of God should stand alone, the love of Christ would compel him to impart God's way and truth to others so as to have co-partners of the same salvation that he himself has received. And even though one hardly gets along with this communication (because the natural man neither understands nor willingly accepts the things of the Spirit of God), one must nevertheless not become weary in patience and intercession, which resists the devil. But God rewards enduring faithfulness. And how could he who has been saved himself see others perish at his side!

Chapter LXVII

The Final Aim of the Manifestation of Christ

February 18, 1841 (Thursday); Evening Meeting
I John 3:11

The final aim of the manifestation of Christ and of the Gospel is that Christ lead men back from the unfriendly relationship of enmity and hatred, into a pleasant, amicable relationship of love and fellowship with God and with each other. Both are inseparably connected with the other: in relation to God, it is faith which overcomes the world and its lust; in relation to men, it is holy brotherly love in which one seeks to please the other for edification. But where the love of the brethren is wanting, there the faith to God is not genuine, for all true children of God are brothers in Christ, united by *one* Spirit in *one* body, and all true believers are also saints and, as such, must consider and treat all believers, as well as themselves too, with all high respect and deference, as vessels of the honor of God, appointed and set apart for His holy service.

If even a rude person shrinks from violating or misusing things that are considered holy in the world and if, for example, King Belshazzar made the measure of his sins full by such degradation of the temple vessels that, in the same night, he and Babel fell into the hands of the Persians, how much more ought we to treat the hallowed vessels of God with holy veneration and reverence, that we may not insult or sin against them and disregard the work of God or ruin it by disrespect. He who considers himself and his fellow members of Christ holy will take care not to desecrate himself or others through sin, but he who does not consider that we are consecrated to God does not mind defiling himself or ruining others through carelessness. However, he who destroys the temple of God (his own body or the church, I Corinthians 3 and 6), him will God also destroy, for the temple of God is holy and we shall not make the members of Christ members of the whore.

Likewise, we shall take heed that we do not hurt or neglect the principal thing, brotherly love, because of secondary things (knowledge) and consequently destroy him whom God has nevertheless accepted and for whom Christ has died (Romans 14) ; otherwise we ourselves are not walking according to love, and place meat or one's own opinion higher than the kingdom of God, which indeed is righteousness, peace and joy in the Holy Ghost. Therefore we shall treasure the work of God in us and in others as the highest thing and protect it by holy brotherly love, and we must also have due regard for the rest of mankind, in consideration of Acts 10: 15.

> "And the voice spake unto him again the second time, What God hath cleansed, that call not thou common."

But it is astounding that precisely the saints and children of God are mistreated, mocked and dishonored most by the unbelieving world, as if they were the worst evil doers. However, just with this sacrilege and wilfulness against the vessels of the grace and honor of God, the children of the devil must fill up their measure of iniquity as vessels of wrath which have been prepared for condemnation.

CHAPTER LXVIII

THE THREE STAGES

February 21, 1841 (Sunday) ; Morning Meeting
I John 3 : 11 ff.

> "For this is the message that ye heard from the beginning, that we should love one another.
>
> "Not as Cain, who was of that wicked one, and slew his brother. And wherefore slew he him? Because his own works were evil, and his brother's righteous.
>
> "Marvel not, my brethren, if the world hate you.
>
> "We know that we have passed from death unto life, because we love the brethren. He that loveth not his brother abideth in death."

John forms three stages: *to love, not to love,* and *to hate.* Love is the case and the nature of the children of God; hate, the method and nature of the children of the devil. In love there is a divine, heavenly fire which warms and fructifies like the sun. Hate is a hellish fire; it destroys and consumes (James 3). The transition from love to hate is formed by the failure of love (not to love), which is coldness and indifference, and even it is just as much opposed to the divine nature as hate itself, for he who does not love is not of God and abides in death. And because in this coldness of death, the flesh already has the upper hand and the devil his sport, from there to hate is therefore a short step and a child of God cannot hover midway between hate and lovelessness.

Hate also has its stages without, at the first onset, leading directly to murder by the hand. Its first outbreaks are caused by the tongue (spoken and written); its words are poison and gall, spears and swords, even though by deceit they appear smoother than butter for hate also takes refuge in pretense, just as Cain first spoke with his brother before he slew him. It is further disclosed in dissension and quarrelsomeness, abuse, slander, lies, calumny, etc. These are the scourges and fiery darts that the wicked one shoots to try all on earth, one after another, and to ignite them with his hellish fire, in which he also succeeds — easily — with all unconverted men because they bear the material for it in them, so that the sinners themselves must fret and ruin one another. The devil uses men as his bow and whoever is not protected by the shield of faith, him his arrows, fiery and poisonous, strike in such a way that he also is set on fire and burns and requites evil for evil.

Hence all the wars and disputes and abominations and accusations in families come into court and upon the battlefield, where *both* contending parties are *equally* wicked and serve the devil and not God because it is not love, but hate, that reigns there. For where the truth of God is found, there the love of God is also and then one does not seize the weapons of the flesh to murder one another in false, blind zeal (like Cain), as it happened at the time of the Reformation. But where there is no love, there the truth is not to be found either.

For children of God are not zealous in a carnal way, neither do they allow themselves to be provoked or embittered to wrath, revenge, enmity; but are gentle in suffering, peaceable, patient, bear all things in love while faith commends all to God (I Corinthians 13), Who judges rightly if we do not ourselves enforce our rights. God does not let us come to shame in this and, besides, we conquer and overcome devilish hatred by divine love (Romans 12:17),

> "Recompense to no man evil for evil. Provide things honest in the sight of all men."

for, in any event, all who are godly are mightier in their nature than are the devilish, although the former seem repressed in this world and, on the whole, are very few in comparison to the children of the devil.

But even though the children of God have to be among lions and dragons in this world, they still may not harm them for Christ gives them power to tread upon serpents and scorpions, that they may go out safely and freely right from the midst of them. A child of God cannot hate, he *must love;* otherwise he is not God's child, and he who has allowed himself to be overtaken by the raging of another fire has much suffering to undergo before he is cleansed again from such defilement.

Chapter LXIX

What Love Is

February 21, 1841 (Sunday) ; Afternoon Meeting
I John 3 : 11 ff.

If we should ask what love is, John answers that in the children of God it is the exact opposite of hate in the children of the devil. As, for instance, hate is not slothful or indifferent but zealous, active, inventive that it allows no rest until its last bit of fury has cooled off, one risks goods and chattels, life and body to secure satisfaction for himself and only then is brought to his senses when he has hurled himself and others into destruction and misfortune and is himself often changed by hardened obstinacy (even as Cain who, after he had slain his brother, asked, "Am I my brother's keeper?"). So is divine love not cold, slothful or indifferent either, but zealous and burning for God and all good things, with resignation and the offering up of one's self, so that every member of the body of Christ cooperates for the edification of the whole and seeks to please all the others for the good and lets one have no rest until the house of God is made ready, like David who would give no slumber to his eyes (Psalm 132) until he had sought out a place for a habitation of God (Isaiah 62 : 6 f.).

> "I have set watchmen upon thy walls, O Jerusalem, which shall never hold their peace day nor night: ye that make mention of the Lord, keep not silence,
> "And give him no rest, till he establish, and till he make Jerusalem a praise in the earth."

Slothfulness and coldness is also the opposite of love,

since in the lukewarmness and drowsiness of the believers the devil exercises his first and greatest power for the destruction of the same, so as to rob the blessing of fellowship and brotherly love, and we shall see to it that we bury not the pound we have received but through usuriousness husband it for the Lord, so that we receive praise from Him and as faithful servants enter into the joy of the Lord on the day of reckoning. For as it is said of Him, "The zeal of thine house hath eaten me up," so shall the love of Christ constrain us also to be zealous for His kingdom and honor, for ourselves and for others, and as good angels of God help and serve one another unto salvation.

Where each one will be for himself only and will go his own way, there neither the love of Christ nor the communion of the Spirit is to be found and he who does not contribute toward the salvation of the whole, does not work out his own salvation either—with fear and trembling. He who does not serve God with fervent love already helps the devil to harm, even if it is not his intention and he does not know it. The influence of the devil through the fleshly mind is very near at hand and by the example of Peter (Matthew 26), we see that even believers and friends with good intentions can serve as instruments of Satan.

Anything that causes slothfulness and uncharitableness and negligence is of the devil and is not God's way. Faith without love's works is dead in itself, even though by word it may boast ever so much. It would indeed be a grievous thing if the children of God were less zealous in love than the children of the devil are in hatred.

February 23, 1841 (Tuesday) ; Evening Meeting
I John 3 : 11 ff.

If one is born of God, love has become his nature, so that he can no longer do otherwise than to love. But it is not a human, partial, variable, whimsical, plaintive love, of which one is not for a moment sure whether it will not suddenly change into the opposite. Instead divine love is a constant, persistent, unchangeable disposition of sincere good will, for as there is no changing or even a trace of variableness in God, so also only a perfect gift comes down from Him, in order that His unchangeable nature may stamp itself upon His children, so that they are not sometimes friendly, sometimes sullen and strange but always like themselves because of love (James 1:17).

> "Every good gift and every perfect gift is from above, and cometh down from the Father of lights, with whom is no variableness, neither shadow of turning."

And as God has undeservingly loved the ungodly, lost sinner-world and has offered up His Only Begotten Son to save it from the dominion of Satan, so also the love of the children of God extends itself impartially to all men, without regard to whether they hate or love us, do us good or harm, whether they deserve it or not, are worthy of love or hatred, i.e., just as they all by nature are (Titus 3:3);

> "For we ourselves also were sometimes foolish, disobedient, deceived, serving divers lusts and pleasures, living in malice and envy, hateful, and hating one another."

for had God looked at it as the proud sinner does, He would indeed have found nothing in the world worthy of love and would have had to reject it.

But His love was a compassionate sympathy, a gracious good will, that He had purposed to Himself (Luke 2:14);

> "Glory to God in the highest, and on earth peace, good will toward men."

however not with the intention that men should remain in their inborn hatefulness (in sin), but that in Christ, His beloved Son, they should actually be presented lovable again, inasmuch as by putting Him on we are changed into His image; for to that end has the Father let His voice be heard from heaven over Christ: "This is my beloved Son, in whom I am well pleased," that by the acceptance of the Same we might attain to divine amicableness. For now the Father *seeks* and also wishes to have such worshippers whom He could love as His children and in whom He could shed His love abroad by the Holy Spirit as an indwelling, living law, by which they would work righteousness and love again and then would be well pleasing to God and men in the dignity of the love of Christ (Ephesians 1:3 ff.) (below), not that by it we would please the world, which, on this account, would rather hate, ridicule and reject us, if we are in Christ and Christ is in us.

> "Blessed be the God and Father of our Lord Jesus Christ, who hath blessed us with all spiritual blessings in heavenly places in Christ:
> "According as he hath chosen us in him before the foundation of the world, that we should be holy and without blame before him in love:
> "Having predestinated us unto the adoption of children by Jesus Christ to himself, according to the good pleasure of his will,

"To the praise of the glory of his grace, wherein he hath made us accepted in the beloved.

"In whom we have redemption through his blood, the forgiveness of sins, according to the riches of his grace;

"Wherein he hath abounded toward us in all wisdom and prudence;

"Having made known unto us the mystery of his will, according to his good pleasure which he hath purposed in himself:

"That in the dispensation of the fulness of times he might gather together in one all things in Christ, both which are in heaven, and which are on earth; even in him:

"In whom also we have obtained an inheritance, being predestinated according to the purpose of him who worketh all things after the counsel of his own will:

"That we should be to the praise of his glory, who first trusted in Christ.

"In whom ye also trusted, after that ye heard the word of truth, the gospel of your salvation: in whom also after that ye believed, ye were sealed with that holy Spirit of promise,

"Which is the earnest of our inheritance until the redemption of the purchased possession, unto the praise of his glory."

Because the devil and the world cannot bear the true, living Christ—especially if the love of Christ compels one to save others as lost sinners from their destruction and to draw them to Christ—the devil then rouses himself up in men with such power that he would fairly devour one alive, and if we do not have a persisting love to the souls for God's sake, like Jesus Who went so far as to die for them, by such "reward" and "thanks" from the world, we will easily be frightened away and do nothing. But even if the world does not recognize and accept us with Christ and the love of God, we nevertheless, as children of God, must unfold such loveliness in our entire character and behavior that at least the Father Himself and all His children must love us and with good pleasure can consider us saints. We must, of course, demand and expect much more of the children of God than of all other men, so that we are not mistaken about them, because two things must meet here and unite in all of them: each one *must love* and also *must be worthy of being loved*.

There is indeed nothing more distressing and more grievous than if one has to see brothers and sisters in Christ with whom one does not know how he stands, who are not lovable in their character and manner and who do not correspond to, but contradict, their holy name and profession, so that one cannot recognize them as children of God or love them as brothers and sisters in Christ as one would like to, and should do. Such incongruity hurts and cannot last. For either we must be lovable as children of God or we must relinquish the holy name of brother or sister, of which we are not worthy if we do not have His Holy Spirit as testimony that we have passed from death to life and have received a perfect gift from the Father of Lights as His children.

When sinners judge one another, none ever think that they themselves are just as hateful and abominable as they whom they judge, and each one sees only the other and not himself (Matthew 7; Romans 2). But with the children of God, in each one the image of Christ must be reflected, so that they recognize and love one another therein as brothers and sisters in Christ, and that they may not offend, but all may edify one another.

Chapter LXX

Brotherly Love; Not Partial

February 25, 1841 (Thursday); Evening Meeting
I John 3:11 ff.

The love of God to His own children is entirely different from His love toward the world—sinners—to whom He only offers His love without their accepting it so as to be saved by it; but in His children He can both dwell and rest as in a possession of His own. Thus also is the love of children of God, from a reciprocal standpoint, entirely different from their love toward the rest of mankind because in the latter, no love toward one another is to be found; but children of God among themselves can and must love because everyone of them has love in him and is lovable in his actions. Holy brotherly love therefore is not partial, i.e., merely for some toward whom one is well disposed and on the other hand slights or hates others; instead it is a divine duty and obligation.

Love also has no law as to how much it ought to do, but is itself a law to those who have it from God, according to which we shall not reckon how much we have done, for love can never do too much. And if we take this law as our standard and besides look to Jesus Who out of love has given His life for us, we never can do enough, for in the sight of God it depends not upon what and how much we do (not upon works or deeds), but upon the disposition in which and by which something is done; whether it is the pure, divine love and good will of the heart, or swaggery and self-righteousness which would like to settle accounts with God, or is kept within limits by reluctance, compulsion and chagrin; for God loves a cheerful giver (II Corinthians 8 and 9).

Christ, therefore, praises the poor widow who gave all she had, even her living, and by that gave more than all the others who, to be sure, had put larger gifts in the treasury. And Paul, likewise, praises the church of Macedonia because they were willing beyond means and would have offered up their lives, first for the Lord and then for the brethren. For even if we out of love did give our lives for our brethren, we still would not have done too much and he who understands the divine method of computation need not fear running short or working to his own disadvantage, in that he does it out of love. For we indeed take nothing of our own, but only of the fulness of God, Who will perform His work through us, so that we shall be nothing more than stewards, helpers, vessels, tools of God and in faith take from above that which we give in charity here below, that God, Who always has enough, may be honored by us.

As with love to the brethren, so with faith to God. It is not what we do (in either respect) that counts or has value in the sight of God, but *how* we do it (the mind of the heart) (according to the example of Abraham). For God does not desire sacrifice from us; rather His good pleasure is in mercy and love, and because love is really sincere good will, our love to God, fundamentally, is nothing else than faith, which, by charity and its works, pours itself out to the brethren (Matthew 25 : 34 ff.).

"Then shall the King say unto them on his right hand, Come, ye blessed of my Father, inherit the kingdom prepared for you from the foundation of the world:

"For I was an hungred, and ye gave me meat: I was thirsty, and ye gave me drink: I was a stranger, and ye took me in:

> "Naked, and ye clothed me: I was sick and ye visited me: I was in prison, and ye came unto me."

For we cannot repay God for what He does for us and if it were otherwise many rich people could think that great things were done and won by their so-called good works, which, without faith to God and love to the brethren, would still count as nothing.

February 27, 1841 (Sunday); Morning Meeting
"im Rohrhof"
Philippians 4: 6 f.

> "Be careful for nothing; but in every thing by prayer and supplication with thanksgiving let your requests be made known unto God.
> "And the peace of God, which passeth all understanding, shall keep your hearts and minds through Christ Jesus."

Be not "careful" but prayerful. Being careful therefore is the opposite of being prayerful. The former is the worship of idols; the latter the worship of God. He who prays cannot be laden with cares; he who is laden with cares cannot pray, for he has no faith in God, no living God (Matthew 6), and the blind, and deaf and dumb idols forsake their blind worshippers right in the time of need, like untrue friends who are not at home when one appeals to them for help. But the living God is not so: He lets Himself be found by those who seek and call upon Him, in distress and at all times.

For if we in the childlike simplicity of faith cast every care and concern upon God, He cares for us and then we are well cared for and have rest and peace instead of the unbearable burden and anxiety of the cares of unbelief.

There is therefore no yoke like Jesus' yoke, so soft that it is light for the bearer because he need have no cares but can pray and tell the Father, Who is very near to all who call upon Him, all that oppresses him. By nature there is no longing and sighing in man for God but only withdrawal and enmity. Therefore God Himself is there, where there is a sincere yearning in us for Him. The reason why unbelievers have such unbearable burdens and misery with their cares, pleasures and sins all their life long and, without conversion, in eternity also, is that men think themselves so great and wise that they must do all things themselves.

Their sins as far as God is concerned are indeed not oppressive to them now, but all the more so their cares, which are so deeply rooted in them that they will not let themselves be loosed from them for anything; and even some who believed for a time become stifled and oppressed by them again because they do not understand the mystery of faith and godliness in which they could find rest for their souls. But the real children of God throw off every burden (Hebrews 12:1) (below) and in their place, in faith take the easy yoke of Christ upon them. Since they have access to the Father they meekly entrust everything to Him and await and receive all help from Him and indeed in such a way that in *their* eyes it is always amazing.

> "Wherefore seeing we also are compassed about with so great a cloud of witnesses, let us lay aside every weight, and the sin which doth so easily beset us, and let us run with patience the race that is set before us,"

But when unbelievers and the ungodly come into distress, they know of nothing to which they can hold. It then happens to them as it did to the priests of Baal with their idols: there is no answer and no attention is paid to them (I Kings 19). And because they despised God in the acceptable time, He does not hear them now, and although they had good days during their entire life, the time of destitution and misery will still come for them after death.

February 27, 1841 (Sunday); Afternoon Meeting (a continuation)

We shall hold nothing earthly or visible as our own and shall not consider ourselves lords either, for we have only *one* Lord and shall be satisfied if only we may be His bondsmen, His servants and stewards, for we have to give account of all that He has entrusted to us, be it wife or children, houses or lands, or even our earthly life. Here nothing is our own: it is the Lord's; but still Christ Himself should and would be our real Possession, Which no one can take away from us, at the right of God. That is why all children of God are and feel like pilgrims in this world, who long for the Upper Homeland and would rather leave this tabernacle to come into the eternal ones.

And we should see to it now that we need not stand outside without shelter when the time of our departure comes and that we do not think carelessly as so many do: "We shall find fellow companions where we are going." The ungodly, of course, have more comrades than the children of God, but that there are many of them is a miserable comfort to those who will be lost. Now if our treasure is on earth, our heart will continue to cling to it as birds to a lime twig from which they cannot get loose.

Therefore, the first condition for acquiring the kingdom of heaven is that one sell everything that he has on earth for it, so that it may not cling to him afterwards and be a hindrance. The heart must be free from the earthly so as to be bound to the heavenly and eternal, that we can soar upwards unhampered and if the temporal is taken from us, we would not on that account deny Christ or be overwhelmed by the grief of the world but would rather thank God and be able to say with Job: "The Lord gave, and the Lord hath taken away; blessed be the name of the Lord."

For if nothing here is our own, we may confidently leave to the Lord as much or as little as He may have entrusted to us, and whether He gives or takes, for to whom much is given, of him much is demanded. But from him who has nothing of the eternal and veritable, even the temporal and perishable that he thought he had shall be taken and the unprofitable servant cast into outer darkness where there will be weeping and gnashing of teeth.

But he who hankers after and will not forsake the earthly can neither have nor retain Christ (the Kingdom of God), but apostatizes in the time of temptation and his work perishes in the fire that God has prepared for us for our proving and purification in this world because a faith of that kind is only human, not divine. Therefore, as men of the world are obliged to insure their alleged earthly possessions that they may not suffer the loss of them, so must we, much more, with divine prudence, be intent upon making our souls secure in the heavenly assurance institution, so that we may not be lost in eternity and, for this, it is necessary that we come to such composure that we can let all things please us and are unmoved in the depths of our heart by the storms and the billows. There the peace of God reigns as king over the entire mind of man and where peace prevails one lives and fares well.

Chapter LXXI

Reciprocal Love, A Characteristic of God's Children

March 2, 1841 (Tuesday); Evening Meeting
I John 3:11 ff.

As the characteristic of the children of God is reciprocal love because they are of God, so the stamp of the children of the devil is reciprocal hatred, but especially towards the children of God. And that is not to be wondered at because the men of the world are of the wicked one, like Cain, so that the whole world lies in wickedness and in its entire Cain-mind, on the whole is an avaricious, earthly-minded Cain-race, upon which the old curse of Canaan also rests, because they are driven by the spirit of the world to do only evil and to hate, and that is not to be wondered at because they themselves are wicked and evil. But this *is,* that they prefer to remain *evil* rather than to become *good* and, through Christ, to let themselves be redeemed from the wicked one.

The children of God, therefore, are well known in the world by their love towards one another, as well as by the hatred and enmity with which they are persecuted by men because they are no longer of the world but of God, and indeed are so separated and set apart from the world that they constitute an unmistakable contrast to it (enter into opposition with it), yet not according to their own choice or bidding but by God's election and calling of grace. However if one of his own strength and on his own account should step out into the battle of the world against the princes and powers of darkness, as did he who said unto Jesus (Matthew 8:19): "Master, I will follow thee whithersoever thou goest," or as Jesus in the form of a parable said of one who would build a tower without first contemplating its cost, or of the king who would go out with 10,000 against one with 20,000 (Luke 14), he would come to shame with his arbitrary, self-chosen undertaking and would reconcile himself anew with the world and make peace.

But if by the renewing of the spirit in him, one is *certain* of his calling and election of God, and goes to the holy war on the side of Christ, he dare not be afraid of the whole world, as great and strong and mighty as it is indeed, that it may swallow him alive, for Christ in him is still greater than the whole world and *He* is not frightened by their number and their cries. And although we are hated and persecuted, beaten, mocked and slandered by the great Cain, we must not let that surprise us but shall think of the Lord Jesus, what happened to Him *on our account* (Hebrews 12) and how He told us in advance that it would and must happen likewise to us in this world in our imitation of Him (John 15; Matthew 10:24, 25b).

> "The disciple is not above his master, nor the servant above his lord."

> "If they have called the master of the house Beelzebub, how much more shall they call them of his household?"

Thus will they also revile our name as an evil, a harmful and a dangerous one against which all must guard themselves, but "rejoice and be exceeding glad (Matthew 5)."

It is strange that the people of the world, who *are* of the devil, calumniate the children of God as fools and devil's children just because the Holy Spirit dwells in them and thereby commit the sin against the Holy Spirit

(I Peter 4), and thus accuse the children of God of being what they themselves are. By no means shall we ever be ashamed, or yield, when we know that we have been chosen and set apart by God Himself and have passed from death to life, for God is mighty to preserve us even in the midst of our enemies, and death we have not to fear.

March 4, 1841 (Thursday); Evening Meeting
I John 3 : 11

John makes a double contrast in that he sets the children of God not only opposite the whole world but also distinguishes the true children of God from the false, counterfeit ones, who have only the appearance of godliness and deny its power because they have not, in truth, broken their way through and passed over from death to life so as to walk in a holy life and to love the brethren. With all their knowledge and prattle, their hearts are cold, uncontrite, earthly-minded, world-like; they prefer the pleasure of the world and the honor of men, to God; they have not died to sin or themselves and would like to satisfy God and the world and stand, so to speak, midway between the two. One would think that they were also believers and converted and yet they are not of God; they are ashamed or afraid to enter into opposition with the world and punish it by word and walk and condemn its works as evil (John 7 : 7; Ephesians 5 : 11),

> "The world cannot hate you; but me it hateth, because I testify of it, that the works thereof are evil."

> "And have no fellowship with the unfruitful works of darkness, but rather reprove them."

so as not to take the reproach of Christ and the enmity and persecution of the world upon them. Because they are not convinced or certain of their being set apart, their calling or election of God, they carry on only their own work and do what seems good to them.

Wherever Christ makes a new start with the Gospel, such half-converted and false believers are to be found, whom one at first does not know (cull wheat *N'Bena*). For a time one had much confidence in them for everything good, but afterwards they become manifest and fail to endure in temptation and trial and fall away because they have no divine foundation or root in them. Some fall away because of the suffering and persecution for the Word's sake; the majority however are destroyed in the time of outward quietude, by the lust of the world, slothfulness, the love of money, etc.

But those who are indeed of God as *the chosen*, nevermore fall away or are ever torn out of the hand of the Father and the Son but remain stedfast in every affliction and temptation for they love Christ more than their own life in the world. They know their high, holy calling and heavenly election of God, by which they have been placed in the world to testify of the light in Christ's stead and name, and are opposed—face to face—by the darkness of the world and do not mind being considered as sheep for the slaughter (Romans 8). For no one is truly converted to God and saved out of the world without just this opposing the world with the testimony of the truth and in this way taking up the struggle with the whole world which seems so much out of proportion if one considers the world great and mighty. But we dare not and shall not be afraid of it for Christ has overcome the world and faith still, as always, overcomes it.

But he who is afraid will be overcome. And why should

we join with the world which hates and persecutes us as soon as we belong to Christ! We therefore have only to be concerned about whether we have actually passed over from death to life so as no longer to fear the death of the body and then we will be happy to be in the world for a time in Christ's stead and to suffer and also to lay down our lives for the brethren and in this way we shall help some to life.

CHAPTER LXXII

THE TWOFOLD DESIGNATION

March 7, 1841 (Sunday); Morning Meeting
I John 3:12 ff.

> "Not as Cain, who was of that wicked one, and slew his brother. And wherefore slew he him? Because his own works were evil, and his brother's righteous.
>
> "Marvel not, my brethren, if the world hate you.
>
> "We know that we have passed from death unto life, because we love the brethren. He that loveth not his brother abideth in death."

"Marvel not, my brethren, if the world hate you." The reason for this hatred is twofold, as it was in the case of Cain. It lies partly in the world because its works are evil and partly in the children of God because their works are righteous, and the light punishes and reveals the darkness and their divine love opposes the hatred of the world and stands in contradiction to it, with the result that the world cannot endure it. For as children of the devil seek their own in the world, so children of God seek that which is Jesus Christ's.

But what is His? *"Behold, all souls are mine;"* saith He (Ezekiel 18:4), and now so much more, since He has died for all and has purchased them with His own blood for a possession, after they, from the beginning, had been snatched away from Him by the devil. But those who abide in sin withdraw themselves from Him as from their lawful Overlord and His death on the cross does not help them because they abide in death.

Hence the saved must be in the world in Christ's stead, must recruit, work and help to rescue men for Christ, Who meanwhile is with the Father—invisible—and until His second coming carries on the redemption work of men through His anointed members in that He uses the believers as a fisherman uses his fishing rod and bait to catch fish. That is why Christ compares the kingdom of heaven to a net that is cast into the sea and gathers all kinds of fish together—good and bad—until it is full. It would indeed then seem that the net (the church of the believers and saints) might be swallowed up by the sea (the world) like the fish-hook is by the fish. Instead others again are caught and saved by it from the destruction of the world and the power of the devil. But of course the believers, out of love to the brethren, must offer themselves up for the cause and be sunk into the sea of the world and of sorrows, for even though not all men will be saved for eternal life, some always are, are chosen and set apart from the world as a peculiar people, and even the few are worth the effort (III John 5 and 6).

> "Beloved, thou doest faithfully whatsoever thou doest to the brethren, and to strangers;
> "Which have borne witness of thy charity before the church: whom if thou bring forward on their journey after a godly sort, thou shalt do well:"

Therefore, the children of God have a twofold role: on the one hand, they are set apart from the world and must keep themselves unspotted by the world and their association with it; on the other, they shall still so influence the world that some will always pass from death to life. In this, all chosen believers must help along and work together by each one doing his part, and are thus called by Christ to missionary work in His stead — without taking their suffering into consideration. For as soon as we support and declare Christ as the Divine Light in word and work, so soon we fare no better among the so-called Christians than the missionaries among the Jews and heathen, since the former just as little know Christ and have passed from death to life as the latter. They are still just as much in death, and do not love the brethren and hate Christ.

Indeed, if one should ask one after the other, in *what* all men are by nature and from which only the saints and believers have been saved, none would know the answer just because they *are* in death. And it is great blindness and folly if one will ask these dead and lost sinners to help with the work and contribute toward saving the lost *heathen* (as it says in a tract from Basel entitled *Persecution of the Christians on the Island of Madagascar*). One cannot help pitying such blind leaders of the blind, who do as the Pharisees of Old did; travel and dispatch missionaries to distant lands and let the men in their midst perish; yes, even delude them with false comfort. They themselves do not enter into the kingdom of God or the life of Christ and those among us who wish to enter, they will not let go in. They lament the blindness and enmity of the heathen towards the evangelists and are themselves opponents of the children of God wherever such among us become known.

By that, one strengthens the nominal Christians in their deception, as if they had passed from death to life, and yet one hates the other. They look for darkness only in the heathen, but as soon as Christ has become *alive in us* and works in love and offers up Himself to save others from death, they clamor about sectarianism, a new faith, etc., and thus the hatred of the world reveals itself here as there because the devil rules the whole world.

Therefore, we have a choice between two things only: either we are actually saved already and then we must offer ourselves up for Christ and lay down our lives for the brethren, or we are still in death and lost and then we ought *first* to be saved ourselves, for fellowship with the saints (I Timothy 2).

Chapter LXXIII

Brotherly Love, The Fruit of the Tree

March 7, 1841 (Sunday); Afternoon Meeting
I John 3:12 ff.

He who does not love is not of God and *abides in death;* he who hates is a murderer, like the devil (John 8:44).

> "Ye are of your father the devil, and the lusts of your father ye will do. He was a murderer from the beginning, and abode not in the truth, because there is no truth in him. When he speaketh a lie, he speaketh of his own: for he is a liar, and the father of it."

Consequently, only *he is of God* who, like God and Jesus Christ, *loves* by offering up himself. True divine love seeks to bring lost men (sinners) to the real salvation of their souls, that they be brought from death to life.

He who himself is still in death cannot work to this end; but he who hates, *kills the souls* of men like a murderer kills the body.

There are two kinds of murder, just as man has a two-fold life, a physical or a soulful one which lies in the blood, and an intellectual one which lies in the spirit of man but which is corrupted in the natural man by sin (the darkness of the devil), so that only fragments and heaps of rubble are left of it, which can express and develop themselves in all kinds of natural talents and powers through practice and education (the languages, the arts, science, and inventions of all kinds). From these ruins of the intellectual life, fallen man constructs all sorts of creations for himself and because of them wonders what he indeed could be and do, and is deceived by this: that he thinks he has a complete intellectual life and, in spite of it, is still an enemy of God and His truth and therefore employs even the intellectual powers that remain, only for evil, in the service of the devil, by whom he is held captive and blinded.

But the spirit of man according to his original designation should know and love God, have fellowship with Him and serve Him, and for this our natural life should merely be the bearer of the outward effect of the good and for the will and honor of God. But in a sinner this is no longer the situation for natural man is *spiritually* dead—without fellowship of God—and for this reason the Son of God has come and died, that He might abolish this spiritual death and, anew, impart His spiritual life to us through His resurrection from the dead and our new birth according to the spirit. For as the spirit of man, by uniting and mingling with the devil (spirit of the world), became darkness and death, so shall it by rebirth out of water and spirit and by reunion with God become light and life, and as darkness expresses itself by hatred and enmity, so light makes itself known by love and peace. This change of the human spirit and mind from darkness to light (from death to life) is established in the holy baptism of the believer because it is a baptism into Christ's death and a being planted with Him in the likeness of His death and resurrection.

Thus the real element of spiritual life consists entirely in love, as the image of God, not in all kinds of knowledge, etc. (which is merely an adornment and adjunct); still much less in the arts and sciences, which deluded men gaze at in astonishment and worship as something great. But precisely this *love* of the brethren which works toward redemption of the lost is that element, just as hate is directed toward harm and is exceedingly fruitful and shrewd in inventions of every conceivable kind of sorcery and torment. However Christ has not come to destroy the souls of men but to save them (Luke 9:56a).

> "For the Son of man is not come to destroy men's lives, but to save them."

March 9, 1841 (Tuesday); Evening Meeting
I John 3:13 f.

> "Marvel not, my brethren, if the world hate you.
> "We know that we have passed from death unto life, because we love the brethren. He that loveth not his brother abideth in death."

According to this advice of the apostle, we should not look for the distinguishing mark of the children of God in anything except *love of the brethren*. Further, all else is merely a deceptive appearance, by which even the divine is changed into poison, when one prefers to aim at great and profound knowledge and, through it, makes learning important to the people (Colossians 3), rather than to insist upon the cleansing and the sanctification of the heart, that the love of God may dwell therein and overflow in all good works. For where love is not found, there knowledge is not of the right kind: it is not the divine truth and wisdom from above but that which is from below and devilish (I Corinthians 8:1 ff.; James 3:13 ff.).

> "Now as touching things offered unto idols, we know that we all have knowledge. Knowledge puffeth up, but charity edifieth.
> "And if any man think that he knoweth anything, he knoweth nothing yet as he ought to know.
> "But if any man love God, the same is known of him."

> _____

> "Who is a wise man and endued with knowledge among you? let him shew out of a good conversation his works with meekness of wisdom.
> "But if ye have bitter envying and strife in your hearts, glory not, and lie not against the truth.
> "This wisdom descendeth not from above, but is earthly, sensual, devilish.
> "For where envying and strife is, there is confusion and every evil work."

So brotherly love is the fruit of the tree which God searches for in His children and Christ longs to have operative in His believers: knowledge of all kinds, however, is merely the leaves which serve as an adornment or a decoration (I Corinthians 13). Therefore, where the divine law of love dwells in the heart, there we find real, divine knowledge and enlightenment also, and in everyone who is born of God, both life-powers — the mind and the heart—are in the right divine order and harmony as the governing knowledge of the truth (the light) and as the accomplishing power for all the good and the acceptable will of God.

But where the mind and the heart are under the influence and in the service of the devil, there is nothing but confusion and disaster, darkness and malice. Then man neither knows nor does the will of God. Thus in the unconverted person the light that guides him is darkness. For this reason his entire life also is evil, and when a person (under the law) would even like to do the good and hates the evil, he cannot yet accomplish it because sin still dwells in him.

But the institution of the law precedes the grace in Christ, so as to direct the will of man toward the good, so that when the Gospel comes and faith brings one to freedom from sin and the powers of accomplishment, he may then direct his heart (the will) to, absolutely and resolutely, do the will of God. And if he then does not do the good, but the evil, it is his own fault because he does not desire the good and, as a result, his will is not in agreement with the will of God (the Father's), but opposes it and that then is one's own sin, which *is* imputed to him, that he does not desire the good but the evil.

The sin of man lies not in the lack of knowledge (the sins that do are the sins of ignorance only, which are not imputed to him), but in the lack of will power: for what shall we think of a person who does not desire to do the good? With the unconverted, that already is his own sin—that he is unwilling to do the good, and it is still much more the case with a pardoned one, who has become *free* in Christ and has been enabled to do the will of God; for had we, at all times and unconditionally, directed our will upon the good, we could always do it and would *never* commit sin. For it is a lie of the devil that holds that a man in Christ *must* sin. A person who indeed wishes to do the good, but cannot, and still does the evil, is not in Christ but under the law (Romans 7), for in Christ there is freedom from sin, and for the will to do good the accomplishment also has come.

March 11, 1841 (Thursday) ; Evening Meeting
I John 3 : 13

How do we feel when we hear the word: "Marvel not, my brethren, if the world hate you"? Have we already experienced something of it too? For the world it is indeed a grievous sign, but for the children of God a good one, and the cause of this hatred of the world lies in the passing over of the children of God from death to life, by which they are parted, singled out, and set apart from the world and form a contrast to it and its hatred by their yearning nature for holiness and charity.

However, just as the divine love of children of God is not an idle word but a fact and the truth, so is the hate of children of the devil not a mere word either, but is accompanied with all the evil works of unrighteousness. And we must learn to keep an eye upon this hatred of the world so that we may not be offended when it strikes us (John 16:1),

"These things have I spoken unto you, that
ye should not be offended."

for every child of God is salted with fire in this world (Mark 9:49).

"For every one shall be salted with fire, and
every sacrifice shall be salted with salt."

Here children of God are accounted as sheep for the slaughter (Romans 8:36);

> "As it is written, For thy sake we are killed
> all the day long; we are accounted as sheep
> for the slaughter."

otherwise, one would not make so much of the hatred of the world for men of the world themselves also hate one another (Titus 3:3),

> "For we ourselves also were sometimes
> foolish, disobedient, deceived, serving divers
> lusts and pleasures, living in malice and envy,
> hateful, and hating one another."

but against those who have passed over, it breaks out in all violence and unrighteousness. They suffer tribulation, anxiety, persecution, famine, nakedness, peril and the sword, without objecting thereto or offering resistance or being permitted to defend themselves, but simply suffer all things patiently out of charity (I Corinthians 13:4).

> "Charity suffereth long, and is kind; char-
> ity envieth not; charity vaunteth not itself, is
> not puffed up."

Men of the world, of course, avenge themselves of the wrong that is done to them; they will not let it come upon them or succumb to it without requital with evil. But the children of God are peace-loving, bear injustice for God's sake, do not vindicate themselves or seek justice in the world because they would not find it anyway. They commit the matter to God and wait patiently for His righteous judgment and their justification on the Day of Christ, for in this world Christ always loses in the proceedings and never wins justice, and the only requital for evil is brought about with good (Matthew 5:38 f.; Romans 12:17).

> "Ye have heard that it hath been said, An eye for an eye, and a tooth for a tooth:
> "But I say unto you, That ye resist not evil: but whosoever shall smite thee on thy right cheek, turn to him the other also."

> "Recompense to no man evil for evil. Provide things honest in the sight of all men."

However the hatred and vengeance of the world toward the children of God is so dreadful that it could easily through fear and terror seduce us to the denial of Christ and apostasy from the truth if we were not provided with the whole armor of God in the evil day.

It is odious to the world that we no longer run with them or do as they, not only with respect to their excessively evil works, but with respect to their idol-worship especially, which they offer as a divine service (I Peter 4), and yet we cannot and may not take part in their works if we have been called of God and have passed from death to life. But as such who, according to the Spirit, now already stand on yonder side and have their real possession there, we dare not fear the hatred and wrath of the world so much since it cannot harm us except in the body and can take nothing from us except the earthly which, anyway, is not our own. For the world does not know what death and life is, but the children of God know that they have passed from death to life because they love the brethren. The world hates us as those who have passed over and, as such, we have nothing to fear but can rejoice and exult triumphantly in all our afflictions.

March 14, 1841 (Sunday) ; Morning Meeting
I John 3 : 14

> "We know that we have passed from death
> unto life, because we love the brethren. He
> that loveth not his brother abideth in death."

Alongside the hatred of the world, holy brotherly love is the only infallible sign of the child of God. Only he who loves the brethren knows that he has passed over from the death of Adam to the life of Christ. All other characteristic of an intellectual life are deceptious and without brotherly love even false (I Corinthians 13), glitter as they will. Divine love is not cold and selfish but devoted and sacrificial, and certainly there is nothing that we can do and repay to *God*. He does not require our service or our sacrifices (Psalms 50 and 51). The world's worship of God with its officiation of formal rites and observances is Cain's sacrifice but God is not served by it: He wants our hearts for His dwelling place. If we would serve God, we must serve the brethren in charity and then God regards it as done to Him and wants to recompense it (Matthew 25).

Without the love of God we are foolish virgins, who indeed had the glowing lamps of knowledge but no oil vessels with them filled with the love of God, just because brotherly love is present only where the passing over from death to life has occurred, where one no longer lives to himself but Christ lives in him. He is not his own lord to do as he would like, for he has become a servant and tool of Christ so as to carry on Christ's work for the salvation of the lost from Satan's power. For as long as men remain dead in Adam's death, so long Christ has not attained the intention of His death upon them, and Christ still comes in the Spirit to give and to sacrifice

Himself for men, and that He desires to do through *us,* if we will let Him live and work in us, so that we no longer live to ourselves but offer up all our time and strength to Him for the salvation of the brethren.

Therefore, *charity* is greater than faith and hope, which temporarily form only the scaffold and the carrier of the spiritual life (of charity) for the time that we shall be here and which will be taken away together with knowledge, the tongues, and the other gifts and powers of the Spirit because only the love of God abides forever, which is to be enjoyed only as the fruit of the Lamb, not as Sodom's apples, which have a beautiful appearance on the outside but inside are full of ashes. However the trees that have only leaves and no fruit are near to the curse (Hebrews 6), for he who does not love is still in the old death because life is found only where there is love. Sacrificial love does not keep accounts and even though it does all that it has been bidden, it ever continues to be obligated to do more and is never finished. But he who loves with his tongue, who insists by word that he loves and still does not have love's works, is a hypocrite and a liar.

Chapter LXXIV

Harmony in Word and Works

March 14, 1841 (Sunday); Afternoon Meeting
I John 3:14

> "We know that we have passed from death
> unto life, because we love the brethren. He
> that loveth not his brother abideth in death."

Now how do we further feel inasmuch as John here, in the name of all children of God, says "We love the brethren"? Is it also true of us? People of the world have something too with respect to one another that they call love. There is seldom a Simon who hates all men without meaning it well with someone (Matthew 5:43).

> "Ye have heard that it hath been said, Thou shalt love thy neighbour, and hate thine enemy."

However, it is not an unselfish, an impartial, a divine love toward all men *for their soul's salvation,* but a partial, selfish, an egotistical love, only for some like-minded whom they are fond of, and as a consequence hate hundreds while they love one, because even the worst people must have someone with whom they can associate and be friendly. Children of God, it is true, cannot love all men either as brothers because brotherly love must be reciprocal and is found only among the saints. But yet their love toward all men is upright and sincere, as the sacrificial love of Christ was toward us all when we were still His *enemies* and dead in trespasses, in that He sacrificed His soul for our souls so as to seek and redeem what is lost.

Thus does Christ still seek and, indeed, generally by means of those to whom He has already revealed Himself as the life. Therefore the redeemed cannot and may not be egotistical, or bear a grudge against anyone at all, not even their worst enemy. And in this we should not readily become weary or lax, even if we do not soon succeed in winning and overcoming our enemies with love, when we consider how unreasonable and how unsympathetic and obstinate we ourselves were until we were persuaded and converted to the mind of the righteous, how longsuffering, how patient and devoted the love of the Lord was in seeking and saving us.

Divine love does not lose heart easily for it is longsuffering, patient; does not let itself become embittered, seeks not its own, thinks no evil, believes and endures and hopes all things. It is concerned only about glorifying Christ with the victories of salvation so that the Father may be praised by reason of His children. We shall work as the *salt of the earth* and as the *light of the world,* for true love is nothing else than *Christ in us* (John 17:26).

"And I have declared unto them thy name, and will declare it: that the love wherewith thou hast loved me may be in them, and I in them."

But if Christ is in us, it then is not a question of what *we* would like to do and have but we give ourselves over to do what the Lord wills, in Whose name we are in the world. Nor dare we be afraid of the great strongholds of the devil in which he opposes us with the most powerful resistance, even if they be the mightiest of this world! A tree does not fall at the first stroke or a stronghold after the first charge and attack. Perseverance is required—especially in prayer and intercession.

Besides, we must declare Christ by word and a walk in the light and take care that we do not take again and destroy with one hand what we would like to give and build with the other, that we offend no one, or by our walk deny what we profess with our lips. Our word cannot be of truth and of blessing when our walk does not harmonize with it. We see the right sacrificial love of Christ in the Apostle Paul, who had wished himself accursed by Christ that he might save his brethren according to the flesh. Thus true, divine love manifests itself in three ways: as a holy brotherly love, as a love toward mankind in general, and as a love toward our enemies in particular.

March 16, 1841 (Tuesday) ; Evening Meeting
I John 3 : 14

The most important thing of the entire Gospel and for every person is the passing over from death to life. That must happen here, during our life in the body, and consists of the divine re-creating and transforming of one's mind and walk, of which natural man knows and has nothing, so that the same person who was once a servant of sin and of the devil, in Christ becomes a servant of righteousness and of God. Every person brings this death with him into the world and carries it about in him until he is converted by the voice of the Gospel.

For the abolition of this first death, Christ, as the Son of man, died in our stead. But His vicarious death does not help those who do not *now* pass over to life, for whoever dies in his sins, without conversion from darkness to light, passes over from the first death (Adam) into the second death and these are all those who are not found in the Book of Life (John 8 : 21 ; Revelation 20 : 15).

> "Then said Jesus again unto them, I go my way, and ye shall seek me, and shall die in your sins : whither I go, ye cannot come."

> "And whosoever was not found written in the book of life was cast into the lake of fire."

It is nothing else than this first death in man that makes men afraid to "die," because the judgment follows thereupon and they have no hope since they have not received the life in Christ because of unbelief. But for him who has passed from the first death to life, there is no further death and he has no fear of dying but joyfully passes out of this miserable life in this wicked world into the invisible world, the sooner the better, because the new life in Christ assures him of the hope of glory (Hebrews 9:27).

> "And as it is appointed unto men once to
> die, but after this the judgment:"

Now, he who does not have the life of Christ's resurrection does likewise not have the fruit of Christ's death, namely, the dissolution of sin through the dying off of the old man, and then one appeals to Christ the Crucified and comforts himself in Him in vain, as does the world, for Christ *out of us* avails us nothing, i.e., if Christ does not *live in us* by the Promised Spirit of Sanctification and Love. For as death is manifest in natural man by unrighteousness and hate, so life is manifested in the children of God by their doing of righteousness and their love of the brethren.

Yet, of all these who are still actually in the old death of sin, there is not a single one who would know or believe or admit that he is in that very condition which the Holy Scriptures call "death." Only the redeemed and those who have passed over from death to life know what death and life is, and it is always a miracle of God before our eyes when one learns to understand it and has the experience. Just for this reason God lets men be told of it— so that they may first take Him at His Word and then experience it themselves and be able to attest to it. Therefore those who do not believe the true God, that they are in death and that He has sent His Son that He might abolish death and bring life, make God a liar and perish in their unbelief, but those who accept the testimony of God in faith will soon experience the truth of it by their own redemption and rebirth.

Therefore, the Lord sent before Him John as the first witness, and those who believe John and acknowledge and deplore their death in Adam need not go far to receive redemption and life, for Jesus follows directly upon the feet of John. They need only turn about, as Mary there (John 20:14), and they will see Jesus, the Risen from the Dead, standing before them in the Spirit, Who translates them from death to life.

> "And when she had thus said, she turned herself back, and saw Jesus standing, and knew not that it was Jesus."

The passing over itself, however, takes place through holy baptism into Christ's death; namely, when the faith of the Word and the knowledge of the truth are present. Therefore infant baptism is nothing more than a deception of the devil because no knowledge of oneself, no repentance and faith has preceded it and accordingly no life in Christ follows.

Chapter LXXV

The Unquenchable Fire

March 18, 1841 (Thursday) ; Evening Meeting
I John 3 : 14 f.

> "We know that we have passed from death unto life, because we love the brethren. He that loveth not his brother abideth in death.
> "Whosoever hateth his brother is a murderer: and ye know that no murderer hath eternal life abiding in him."

The sign of the new *life* is *love*: the proof of the old death is hate. Love is God Himself and true blessedness; hate is a dark power of the devil in natural man—and misery, and he who here does not come forth from the first death to life by believing the Gospel, will nevermore come out of it afterwards (for a spirit cannot be annihilated) ; it is rather an eternal *continuance in damnation,* where men feel and are conscious of their misery in the torment and agony thereof: *"Where their worm dieth not, and the fire is not quenched* (Mark 9)*."*

As for ourselves, we can best know the meaning of eternal damnation by considering what the first death is, in which the people are *now.* Most people, of course, pass their lives in a great deal of activity of body and spirit, but their *spirit is dead* in relation to God because they do not know God and have no fellowship with Him, but hate Him and men, and like downright tormentors and devils destroy one another. The death of men is therefore not a non-existence but a state of existence, in a wretched condition however. For when an animal dies, it ceases to exist because its life lies only in its blood and has no spirit; but when a person dies according to the body, his existence, for that matter, does not come to an end because his spirit cannot die; instead the death of the spirit subsists in the dark power: hate and enmity, and even *now* man bears the worm and fire, hell, in himself and because of it life on earth becomes an entrance to hell.

The worm lies in the *evil conscience,* which eats and gnaws and cries damnation. But now the unsaved try to drown the *inward* cries of the conscience by *outward* cries and clamor and the intoxication of sensual lust, as Israel had drums beaten in the Valley of Hinnom (Gehenna) so as not to hear the screaming of their burning children. But nevertheless they must once hear these condemning voices as a continual lamentation and accusation without being able to flee from them through all eternity: "Woe unto you! You could have been saved but you would not!" because their worm does not die. That is the *one* side of damnation; the *other* side is the fire that is not quenched.

In this life, the hellish fire enters into the hearts of the ungodly. It boils up in them like an erupting volcano and belches forth in streams of unrighteousness and ungodliness from throat and mouth, and can find no rest, day or night, from destroying themselves and others. The indwelling hatred breaks out in enmity, disputation, contention, strife, envy, malice, lust of the flesh, lust of the eyes, excesses in eating and drinking, etc. That is the tongue which is set on fire of hell (James 3), for all the evil that brings the soul into hell proceeds from the heart (Matthew 15). But in eternity this fire becomes unquenchable since no further satisfying of it is possible, for the resurrected body no longer is material or physical like the present mortal body, but immortal and imperishable like that of the righteous.

On the other hand, the blessedness of the children of God subsists in complete, uninterrupted *love,* in a union with God, because all are of one heart and one soul, and no enmity of the devil is present, through whose influence our blessedness now is so frequently disturbed and saddened; but not until the Millenium of Christ will it be made perfect for the firstborn and after that, in eternity, for all the redeemed, by the *removal* of Satan. It is for this reason that we must now strive to be redeemed from the dark power of the devil and be transplanted into the life of Christ.

But anyone who comes to his senses and to *conversion,* must also, for a time, hear the voice of condemnation in his conscience; however the bad conscience is soon changed into a good one and if he then purifies his heart as well, he no longer will hate, but will love the brethren as himself.

Chapter LXXVI

Faith in the Promise

March 19, 1841 (Friday) (from a meeting in Faellanden)
Luke 1 : 45

> "And blessed is she that believed: for there
> shall be a performance of those things which
> were told her from the Lord."

Mary, the chosen mother of the Savior, is a fine example of faith for all believers, to whom this beatitude also applies. Mary did not know how it should come about in a natural way that she should become a mother without a man's participation for that runs counter to the course of nature and is impossible. However, she believed the promise which was given to her of God and did not doubt in unbelief, but glorified God with the perfect assurance that what He promises He is mighty to perform.

It happens likewise to everyone who shall be born again, or in whom Christ shall be born: the promise of God and the faith of man must meet so as to bring forth this miracle of God. For no one can be born anew except the one who has recognized himself in his old nature as being an ungodly, a dead and lost soul. For it would not require a special promise of God if it might come about naturally and no one can believe the promises of God when they absolutely oppose nature and contradict reason as being something impossible, except only the one who has recognized himself as being nothing and of utter incapability.

Therefore, the promise of God is not given unconditionally to all men without distinction, but only to those who believe in hope against hope. In the face of that, the question, "How shall this come about that a sinner and ungodly one may become a child of God and an heir of salvation," always arises. This, of course, dead sinners think about least of all and it causes not a scruple among them, for they imagine that it is self-understood that they are children of God and will be saved.

But this their father the devil—the liar—has invented, that an ungodly one shall not doubt his sonship of God or his salvation. But God surely would not have sent His Son into the world if men already, as sinners, were children of God and could be saved; rather the first thing God accomplishes in man for his salvation is that he begins to doubt this very theory and out of this doubt a struggle of life and death evolves, even to the point of despair in himself. Only then comes the good news and there, where, from a human standpoint, all is at an end and lost, faith in the gracious promise of God appears and to this faith the promise is affirmed and fulfilled by impartation of the Holy Spirit. For no one is a child of God except through Jesus Christ the Son.

However, if it is Christ Who is in us, then it is no longer a question what one, by and of himself, is able to do with respect to a holy life, for what man cannot do, that Christ most certainly can: and there is no doubt that Christ can lead a holy life. If we would but receive Christ as that for which He was made for us of God (I Corinthians 1:30), a holy life of itself would result.

> "But of him are ye in Christ Jesus, who of God is made unto us wisdom, and righteousness, and sanctification, and redemption:"

But Christ cannot live in us so that we can be saved unless the old death of sin has first been abolished and that, again, cannot be destroyed in us unless we, at a time before, have recognized and felt it an impossibility. To God alone is all praise and honor due for His grace and Mary's song of thanksgiving is then in effect.

> ". . . My soul doth magnify the Lord,
> "And my spirit hath rejoiced in God my Saviour.
> "For he hath regarded the low estate of his handmaiden: . . ."

Chapter LXXVII

Both Divided and Mixed!

March 21, 1841 (Sunday); Morning Meeting
I John 3: 14 f.

> "We know that we have passed from death unto life, because we love the brethren. He that loveth not his brother abideth in death.
> "Whosoever hateth his brother is a murderer: and ye know that no murderer hath eternal life abiding in him."

A child of God who has rightly broken his way through to God cannot possibly be both divided and mixed—between death and life, hate and love, darkness and light, righteousness and sin, Christ and Belial—but must on the whole do righteousness and, from within and without, wrestle against every defilement and intermixture with evil (II Corinthians 6).

But not all who become believers and receive the beginning of the life in Christ are so completely minded in Christ. For as *hard* as the passing over from death to life is, so easy is the passing over or back-step from life to death because the boundary line between the two is unnoticed, and man of himself is more inclined to evil than to good because the deceit of sin is so subtle. Of course, whoever has forced his way through definitely stands on the side of Christ and no longer yields to the way of the murderer, no longer is inclined to the evil but to the good. But he who is only half-converted remains standing on the boundary, between death and life, and wavers continually: 'He has the name that he lives and yet is dead.'

They have indeed seen, heard, tasted and felt *something* of eternal life, of the powers of the future world; i.e., insofar as eternal life consists in the knowledge of God (John 17). But they do not have eternal life abiding in them and do not endure in the truth because it is more learning than power of life. Generally they fall away already in this life, or even though they should maintain an appearance of godliness to the end, they will still fall down in the judgment.

They are those whose spirit always opposes anything that is said of a perfect, sinless life in Christ. They do not believe that men in this world can attain to living holy like Christ. Accordingly they want to be divided and mixed, between good and evil (for they do not want to be entirely evil either and even much less entirely good) and since there are many of them, it is necessary for us to ponder well whether we have actually passed over from death to life or are still standing on the border and begin to whore in the land of Moab and are not coming into possession of the Promised Land. One then permits all kinds of sins to himself, counting upon the righteousness of Christ and His blood, and yet Christ has died that He not only lead us out of Egypt but also bring us into possession of the Promised Land; namely, into possession of *our own heart*, which is not otherwise in our power to work righteousness, but is possessed by Satan.

However, through the death of Christ and His resurrection and by our being planted together with Him in holy baptism, we are made free from Satan's power, to possess and govern ourselves, as in the service of Jesus Christ for righteousness, in which the true spiritual freedom subsists. Then we must be on our guard, if we have passed over Jordan and have come into possession of the Promised Land, that we not let the old inhabitants live or allow ourselves to become allied with them, but annihilate them by root and branch. Otherwise they will later become a snare and pitfall to us again, that we no longer abide in grace and, because of them, are driven out from possessing the Promised Land, as Adam was from Paradise and Israel from Canaan.

It happens thus to all who have not been converted rightly and have not passed rightly from death to life, that the surviving destroyer becomes their master again. Therefore we must actually go out to war against the Canaanites; then the Lord will go out with us and deliver them into our hands, and he who thus purifies his heart *here* and keeps it from every defilement of the flesh and the spirit, will afterwards come into possession of the promised inheritance.

It is true, children of God can also err, in over-haste, but not from habit or from malice, and as soon as they become aware of their error, they immediately clear it away by voluntary confession, before the accuser anticipates them. They do not let the sun go down upon it, much less do they hide it for days, weeks, months (Matthew 7:21).

"Not every one that saith unto me, Lord, Lord, shall enter into the kingdom of heaven; but he that doeth the will of my Father which is in heaven."

Chapter LXXVIII

The Voluntary Sacrifice

March 21, 1841 (Sunday); Afternoon Meeting
I John 3:16

"Hereby perceive we the love of God, because he laid down his life for us: and we ought to lay down our lives for the brethren."

In what school must we learn the love of God? Only from God Himself can we learn it: "Hereby perceive we the love of God, because he laid down His life for us." If we should ask: "Why has Christ sacrificed His life for us?" the answer is:

(1) Because by nature we are hopelessly lost;

(2) Because He would not have us perish in this way He had to lay down His life for our life, to ransom us and make us free from Satan's unrightful lordship, if we will accept this ransom for our souls.

If we should further ask: "What moved the Lord to such devotedness?" the answer is "His own compassion, His spontaneous love!" For nothing except His compassion on our misery could force Him to that end; He would not permit us to be lost eternally in the death of Adam. We have *Him* alone to thank when anyone is saved (Hebrews 2:9 f.; 5:9),

"But we see Jesus, who was made a little lower than the angels for the suffering of death, crowned with glory and honor; that he by the grace of God should taste death for every man.

"For it became him, for whom are all things, and by whom are all things, in bringing many sons unto glory, to make the captain of their salvation perfect through sufferings."

"And being made perfect, he became the author of eternal salvation . . . ;"—

however, not unconditionally for all men, although God desires that all should be saved and come to the knowledge of the truth (I Timothy 2). His death in and by itself does not save us unless we become obedient to Him in faith and accept the salvation that He—by it—has won for us. To bring them to the obedience of faith (Romans 1), is the reason why the merciful God lets the good news be proclaimed to lost sinners. But this acceptance must come about voluntarily, like the fall and disobedience of Adam and the resignation and self-sacrifice of Jesus were voluntary (John 10:17).

"Therefore doth my father love me, because I lay down my life, that I might take it again."

Now, wherever this Gospel of Christ is preached, the kingdom of God has drawn nigh to men, so that they *can* be saved if they desire to be (Luke 10:11).

"Even the very dust of your city, which cleaveth on us, we do wipe off against you: notwithstanding be ye sure of this, that the kingdom of God is come nigh unto you."

This overwhelming proof of the love of God and Christ

toward us — sinners — should melt our hearts away. Otherwise nothing has any penetrating power. Yet he who hears about it and does not believe, will not be redeemed from Satan's power but will abide in death, and because eternal life consists in knowing the only true God and Him Whom He has sent, Jesus Christ, it is indeed possible that many have received the beginning of this life and still do not have it *abiding* (dwelling) in them if they do not let their hearts be purified from every sin. In this respect, many will find themselves misled by the old hymn: *"Christi Blut und Gerechtigkeit ist mein Schmuck und Ehrenkleid,"* etc. (Jesus' blood and righteousness is my robe and glorious dress), who still have never looked into the mystery of Christ's death for us, the cause of which is our death descending from Adam, the intention however, our salvation from this first death. And wherever this proof of the love of Christ penetrates through to conversion of man, there it produces the same love in us toward the brethren.

Just as Christ has not paid gold and silver for our ransom from sin and the power of Satan but has laid down His own blood (His soul) for us, so must we also lay down our souls for the brethren and we shall not think that this is done by visible oblations if the souls of men are to be saved from death. Only then has witnessing for Christ a saving power, when the witness can offer himself up as a sacrifice for it: for he who is fearful of men for his own life in the world or for whatever else he has (wife and children, house, lands, etc.) cannot deliver the Word of Christ in purity and sincerity to men so that they can understand or attain to the purpose of Christ's death, because men by nature do not know—or believe—that they are the devil's and without that no *conversion* from Satan's power to God is possible. But he who *without fear* professes the beatific truth ("not as the scribes") will indeed be hated, persecuted and martyred by men on that account; yet just in the offering up of his soul for Christ, he accomplishes something for the kingdom of God—for the salvation of some from death and destruction—for nothing has a penetrating saving power like the *Word of Truth.*

That is why those who seek their own honor and love their own life cannot work or conquer for Christ, for they falsify the Word of God and create another gospel and way to salvation, and instead of witnessing to all men that Christ has died to save all from the death of sin who are obedient to Him, and that holy baptism into the death of Christ has this significance and effect when faith has preceded it, they falsely say and vainly comfort thus: "Original sin rests upon infant children until they are baptized; consequently, without baptism they cannot come into the kingdom of God." (That is what a famous pastor preached recently.)

March 23, 1841 (Tuesday); Evening Meeting
I John 3 : 16

> "Hereby perceive we the love of God, because he laid down his life for us: and we ought to lay down our lives for the brethren."

Now if we shall love, it is necessary for us to know in what love consists, and that we see in the love of Christ toward us, inasmuch as He, as the Lord of All, left His glory with the Father, became a Son of man and in obedience unto death upon the cross laid down and poured out His soul for us, as a sacrifice and ransom for *our* souls— He, as the guiltless and unblemished Lamb of God, took the sin in Adam upon Himself for all men, to reconcile us, to abolish the right and claim that Satan, on account of sin, has upon us, and to purchase freedom for the captives. Without this ransom which Christ paid to Satan for our souls, all men would have to be lost forever. For this, the Righteous One had to offer up Himself as the sacrifice for the unrighteous. This however could not have come to pass if the Son of God had not become a Son of man, had not taken upon Himself a human soul in order to shed His blood to purify and sanctify our souls from sin by it. But because Christ was without sin, Satan had nothing in Him and He for that reason could reconcile and redeem us with innocent blood.

But Satan is all the less likely to lose his lawful claim upon him who abides in sin since it now depends upon man's own choice whether he will accept the ransom of Christ or remain in sin and the power of Satan. So it is no longer fate, because God will not condemn man on account of Adam's guilt, but each one only on account of his own unbelief in the presence of salvation in Christ. Neither can anyone merely claim reconciliation in Christ because Christ died and shed His blood for the forgiveness of sin, and then, despite it, continue to abide in sin, for the blood of Christ is the ransom for our souls. But he who serves sin is not free, neither can he love God, nor himself, nor the brethren, for by committing sin man becomes his own murderer in the hand of the devil.

The whole institution of the salvation of Jesus Christ has no other aim than to cleanse and to free us from sin, and since He accomplished this out of love to us, only he *loves himself* who lets himself be redeemed from sin by Christ so as to lead a holy life for God in this world. But whoever does not truly love himself so as to save *his soul* from death, cannot love the brethren either, for he who is still in the power of the devil himself cannot save *others* out of it. Hence each one himself is actually his own *neighbor* where the salvation of the soul is concerned, but he who really loves himself must also love the brethren as himself.

Yet he whom the love of Christ constrains to save himself and others, unavoidably encounters the hatred and enmity of the world and the devil, so that we cannot otherwise truly love the brethren unless we are able to lay down our souls for them, even as Christ has laid down His soul for us, in order to win us, and this propitiatory sacrifice of Christ indeed ever remains a mystery to us: we cannot perceive how it could happen that our souls could be redeemed and healed by the out-poured soul of Christ. But he who accepts this good message in faith will soon experience the truth of the same by the great change that takes place in him, that he need no longer serve sin and is able to serve righteousness.

CHAPTER LXXIX

THE MIRACLE OF LOVE

March 25, 1841 (Thursday) ; Evening Meeting
I John 3 : 16

> "Hereby perceive we the love of God, because he laid down his life for us: and we ought to lay down our lives for the brethren."

How can we come to understand the proof of Jesus' love for us in His dying? What does His death avail us? This might seem a foolish question when one only blindly and in general accepts and repeats that the death of Christ was gain for the world, without each individual one giving account of it to himself just how His death has benefited him. —Has it saved *me* from the death of Adam and translated me into the life of God? Has the death of Adam with all its consequences, namely sin, really been abolished in *me* through the death of Christ so that Satan has nothing more in me (II Timothy 1:9; Hebrews 2:14)?

> "Who hath saved us, and called us with an holy calling, not according to our works, but according to his own purpose and grace, which was given us in Christ Jesus before the world began,"

> "Forasmuch then as the children are partakers of flesh and blood, he also himself likewise took part of the same; that through death he might destroy him that had the power of death, that is, the devil;"

For when the death of Christ has once been fulfilled in power in us, we must then *ourselves* be able to search and to know whether *Jesus Christ is in us;* otherwise we are inefficient and rejected (II Corinthians 13:5).

> "Examine yourselves, whether ye be in the faith; prove your own selves. Know ye not your own selves, how that Jesus Christ is in you, except ye be reprobates?"

It seems indeed as if the death of Adam with all its consequences had not been undone by Christ's death, since the saints and children of God in this world are still subject to suffering in the flesh and also to the death of the body, like all other people, and, to be sure, death is the last power of the enemy over them (Romans 8; I Corinthians 15), but we nevertheless, of good hope and with great certitude, say that the death of Adam *with* all its consequences has been undone by the death of Christ for the believers and elect of God.

For as far as the sufferings of this time are concerned, we know that they no longer are a punishment and curse for sin to the children of God but a blessing and good thing for their purification, and that corporeal death no longer is anything evil and dreadful for them either but something good and agreeable because in them is fulfilled what is written: "O death, where is thy sting?" (I Corinthians 15; John 11). For the sting of death which terrifies the unbelievers is sin and that is destroyed in the children of God, but not for the world since the world *abides* in Adam's death and consequently in the devil's power, and Christ's death avails them nothing, as much as they would blindly like to depend upon the fact that Christ died for the forgiveness of sin and take comfort in it. Christ did, of course, die for all, however not so that men should abide in sin and Adam's death, but so that they *should all live unto Him* Who has died and risen for them (II Corinthians 5: 16 f.).

> "Wherefore henceforth know we no man after the flesh: . . .
> "Therefore if any man be in Christ, he is a new creature: . . . "

Therefore, the world is deceived with its false comfort of Christ's death, for Christ pledged His soul as a ransom for His sheep from the devil's power. But the unbelievers are not Christ's sheep because they do not obey His voice and He cannot give them everlasting life (John 10), so that, in the end, only the *sheep of Christ* have the real benefit of the death of Christ, that they nevermore perish and that no one can pluck them out of the hand of God, for, since they know Christ and have life in Him, they follow no other voice, and if a thousand seducers should come, because they know that they have come from death to life and that there is no other life than that life which Christ has given them.

But the world does not know this and is therefore exposed to the seduction of anyone at all. Thus one sees how the *same people* who commit all kinds of foolishness and ungodliness in their daily life, and especially at their national festivals, then want to observe religious celebrations too, to honor Christ and by that carry on their mockery of them. But if the people considered the death of Christ according to its real purpose, there would be many who would have to be astonished and frightened at an examination of themselves if they were asked: "Have you really received the unending benefit of the death of Christ? Have you come from the death of Adam to the life of Christ?", etc.

March 28, 1841 (Sunday); Morning Meeting
I John 3:16 ff.

> "Hereby perceive we the love of God, because he laid down his life for us: and we ought to lay down our lives for the brethren.
> "But whoso hath this world's good, and seeth his brother have need, and shutteth up his bowels of compassion from him, how dwelleth the love of God in him?
> "My little children, let us not love in word, neither in tongue; but in deed and in truth."

He for us, the Lord for the subjects, the Creator for the creatures, the Shepherd for the sheep, the Righteous for the unrighteous! The miracle of love, which we shall look into and appreciate fully, really lies in the *incarnation* of the Only Begotten Son of God, in consequence of which we must reverence the love of the Father in sending Him as well as the love of the Son to us in lowering Himself (Philippians 2), as aforetime He was with the Father in glory, which glory He left of His own free will and, for it, "took upon himself the form of a servant, . . . and became obedient unto death, even the death of the cross." *Not* as the Pharisees say, that he was born like an ordinary man and was lifted up and deified as the Son of God afterwards (in consideration of Luke 1:35,

> "And the angel answered and said unto her, The Holy Ghost shall come upon thee, and the power of the Highest shall overshadow thee: therefore also that holy thing which shall be born of thee shall be called the Son of God."

where it is said merely that the Man Jesus Christ was the Son of God); but *because He received the humanity appropriated to Him in conjunction with His divine nature* so as to bring us in Him Himself to fellowship with God, if *we* accept Him as He has accepted our human nature upon Himself so as to die as a sacrifice for sin and, by this means, purify and redeem *our* human nature from the sin in Adam. Upon His incarnation death followed of itself, for He had come into the world for that purpose, to die for us and, by His death, abolish sin.

Had He desired to teach only, He would not have come Himself (Matthew 21:33),

> "Hear another parable: There was a certain householder, which planted a vineyard, and hedged it round about, and digged a winepress in it, and built a tower, and let it out to husbandmen, and went into a far country:"

but would have sent His messengers and servants as was done so many times under the Old Testament;

> "God, who at sundry times and in divers manners spake in time past unto the fathers by the prophets,"—Hebrews 1:1

speak, He can also through His ambassadors and prophets; but die for our sins He must Himself, if we should be helped from everlasting death. He who considers Him only a Teacher does not know Him as God's Son.

That is why Jesus gave to Nicodemus insight into this mystery of the necessity for the redemption of sinners through His sacrifice for us. For our rebirth is connected in the closest way with the death of Christ (John 3); the former is the purpose of the latter. Without our new birth the death of Christ avails us nothing, for Jesus had to take on our human nature so as, through His death, to cleanse it from sin and make us fit for a union with God, because no sinner or unclean one has any inheritance in the kingdom of Christ and of God. Therefore God exalted Him (as the Son of man), that at the name of Jesus every knee shall bow and every tongue shall confess Him Lord. He took upon Himself the same human nature that we received by birth, so as to feel exactly as we feel and be "in all points tempted like as we are, yet without sin," so that He might, just therein, help us.

This human state of mind caused Jesus such agony and struggle that He quaked and trembled before the end He should accomplish in Jerusalem (Luke 12:50; John 12:27; Matthew 26:37).

> "But I have a baptism to be baptized with; and how am I straitened till it be accomplished!"

"Now is my soul troubled; and what shall I say? Father, save me from this hour: but for this cause came I unto this hour."

"And he took with him Peter and the two sons of Zebedee, and began to be sorrowful and very heavy."

Notwithstanding, it was not a doubtful wavering in His resolution to die for us, and we shall not be offended at this human state of the mind of Jesus, for He should and would be like one of us in His days in the flesh and not higher. He suffered and died, *not as the Son of God but as the Son of man,* in our stead, and His death was not an ordinary death of man but the expiatory sacrifice for the sin of the world, and if, in following Him, we in turn must also lay down our souls for the brethren, it would not have the character of reconciliation and redemption but would be a testimony of the truth of the Gospel, for we cannot repay Christ for His love unless we repay it to the brethren, out of love to Him, so that we may save some.

Chapter LXXX

Gold or Straw

March 28, 1841 (Sunday); Afternoon Meeting
(a continuation)

To understand rightly why Jesus pledged His soul for our souls, one must have recognized himself as a dead sinner, condemned by the law. Otherwise one misuses the love of God and of Christ to his own destruction, for the world, in its way, would like to have part in the sacrifice of Christ too. It esteems it very lightly, sugars a pill with it and still abides in sin—in death, in enmity against God, in the disposition of the flesh, in the power of the devil— and yet the only purpose of the appearance of Jesus Christ in the flesh and of His death on the cross is clearly expressed in the words of the angel (Matthew 1), "Thou shalt call his name JESUS: for he shall save his people from their sins."

But those whom the vicarious sacrifice of Jesus *really concerns* are such only who, by the preliminary work of the law, in their own estimation acknowledge themselves as being so wretched and ungodly, dead, unworthy and incapable that they feel they dare not apply it to themselves and, as ungodly ones, consider themselves righteous by mere faith in the vicarious death of Christ on the cross because He was put under the law in order that He might ransom those *under the law* from the curse, and that they might, because of it, receive the blessing of the sonship of God. For as hard as it is to bring proud sinners to the knowledge that they *as sinners* cannot be saved, because sinners are not of God but of the devil from whose power they must first be converted, so hard it is also for those under the law to believe that they *as ungodly men are justified* in Christ and yet the exchange is not effected otherwise than by faith itself.

By faith, the old man of sin must be put off and die with Christ in such a way that he cannot afterwards come into his rights again, so that the new man in Christ may not be detracted from the way of God and Christ or be detained upon it from following in His footprints. To explain, the new man in Christ may no longer love his life in this world but must hate it and bring it as an offering for the true spiritual, eternal life, lest the devil rob us again and to this end attack us with the earthly, and if we then love our souls and seek to save them here, we lose them *eternally;* but if we can lose them here, we save and win them eternally (Matthew 16; John 12; Luke 14).

Jesus uses the expressions "soul" and "life" interchangeably. We should not think when John says that we ought to lay down our lives for the brethren, that we, on that account, must *love the brethren more than we love ourselves,* for we must be able to lay down our souls here so that *we can save ourselves* and gain them in eternity. And if we cannot do it for the brethren (i.e., for Christ), we cannot do it for ourselves either. In this fire of trial and purification, it is revealed whether our faith is divine or human—whether it is gold or straw. The real and true purgatory fire is in this world, not in the future one (I Corinthians 3). Our earthly life is nothing more than a cloak by which we are now covered and which we, in any case, must once *take off* so as to disclose what is hidden thereunder, whether the old man—hypocrite and sinner—or the new man of God—Christ.

If the Latter lives in us, we need not be afraid to remove our cloak and, in case of an extremity, shall willingly leave it in the hand of the whore and adulteress (like Joseph), so as to preserve our *souls chaste* unto everlasting life, and we shall not be frightened even if the devil heats the furnace of affliction in this world seven times hotter, or refrain from confessing Christ and His truth, for in the end not even the smell of fire will have passed upon the faithful witnesses as though they had ever been in the furnace.

April 4, 1841 (Sunday); Morning Meeting
I John 3 : 16 ff.

"Hereby perceive we the love of God, because he laid down his life for us: and we ought to lay down our lives for the brethren.

"But whoso hath this world's good, and seeth his brother have need, and shutteth up his bowels of compassion from him, how dwelleth the love of God in him?

"My little children, let us not love in word, neither in tongue; but in deed and in truth."

The apostle obviously intends to show us how and what we ought to learn of Jesus as our Lord and Master; namely, as on earth each apprentice learns what he has a delight in and enters upon an apprenticeship of that particular master who can teach him *what* he desires to learn, so that he may learn everything that his master knows and does, and in time he too becomes a master. Thus must we enter the apprenticeship of Jesus and *learn* of Him, what He, as the Son of man, followed and practised on earth; namely, self-denial, obedience to the will of God, and blessedness. For this He is the *only Master*. But he who has neither the desire nor the inclination thereto does not enter His apprenticeship and does not learn these things; nor can anyone come to Him unless the Father draws him (John 6).

With respect to spiritual things, there are only two teachers and masters for mankind. The one is the devil from whom we learn the evil, who has many apprentices and companions, and the entire world is his workshop. Things clink and clank from it everywhere. The Other is Jesus, but of Him we must learn not merely to create worlds or to walk on the sea, but to do righteousness and to exercise love and be humble. Nor is it intended by that, that one learn to drive out devils, do great things, preach, etc. All that does not make the disciple of Christ, if, with it, one still commits sin and does unrighteousness (Matthew 7:21), even though he should call Him Lord and Master.

> "Not every one that saith unto me, Lord, Lord, shall enter into the kingdom of heaven; but he that doeth the will of my Father which is in heaven."

The real trade and profession that Jesus followed on earth was to do good, etc. (Acts 10:38).

> "How God anointed Jesus of Nazareth with the Holy Ghost and with power: who went about doing good, and healing all that were oppressed of the devil; for God was with him."

This we must learn of Him. Then in addition we can indeed still learn many other things of Him; for instance, to drive out devils (Luke 10:17 ff.), but that does not save us.

> "And the seventy returned again with joy, saying, Lord, even the devils are subject unto us through thy name.
>
> "And he said unto them, I beheld Satan as lightning fall from heaven.
>
> "Behold, I give unto you power to tread on serpents and scorpions, and over all the power of the enemy: and nothing shall by any means hurt you.
>
> "Notwithstanding in this rejoice not, that the spirits are subject unto you; but rather rejoice, because your names are written in heaven."

There are two byways from the right way of life. The one (to the right) teaches the people that if they only believe on Christ the Crucified it is good enough; it does not depend upon *works*, etc. The other (to the left) holds that one needs but to live honestly and respectably (do what is right) and he will not come amiss. But both are equally far removed from the true way and goal. Those of the former lay the foundation but build no further; these of the latter build without a foundation. For, as there is no other way to salvation except by faith in the blood of Christ for the forgiveness and cleansing of our former sins, the house must then also be built upon this foundation if the death of Christ shall accomplish its purpose in us, and although His obedience, devotedness and self-sacrifice even to death on the cross on the one hand have certainly come to pass for our *reconciliation,* these characteristics then, on the other hand, just as certainly are still our examples which we must imitate and follow and conform to. For if our old man has actually died with Christ and has been planted together with Him in the likeness of His death, then the same can no longer hinder us from becoming, also with our life, a sacrifice for Christ.

But with this, namely that one believes Jesus died for the reconciliation of our sins, one has not yet entered the apprenticeship of Christ. Merely with that we are not yet scholars and disciples of Jesus for the purpose of learning His profession, what He did and *alone* can do and teach. For in addition to the true Teacher and only Master, there are, of course, still great numbers of false masters and teachers in the world, against whom we must be on our guard should they present themselves as preachers of righteousness, and unless we learn of Jesus, as disciples, what *He* has done (Romans 8:7), we are not Christians.

> "Because the carnal mind is enmity against God: for it is not subject to the law of God, neither indeed can be."

But *that* is this: In following Him we must *lay down*

our souls for the *brethren.* To this we are debtors. And if we have died with Christ to love of self, to selfishness, to vainglory and indulgence of the flesh, the offering up of our life no longer seems so difficult to us; and even though we still, at all times, have a battle and notice resistance on the part of the sensuous man and must deny ourselves things that are far more dear and precious to us than our earthly life,* the spirit nevertheless rules over the flesh; otherwise it could not be done and then no one could have eternal life (Christ) in him and be saved.

Not that we deserve anything for having laid down our lives for the brethren for there is no merit in doing what one is obliged to do. But if we do *not* do it or cannot do it for the brethren, we do not have Christ in us as the *eternal life* and, besides, to begin with, it would appear to be a matter of one's own salvation. But men are generally concerned most about what one ought to learn of Christ, not unlike the boys at Bingen, when the inspector asked who wanted to learn to become a worth while person, none aimed any higher than at their earthly calling. Men have either no idea at all about "salvation" or only an absurd one.

April 4, 1841 (Sunday); Afternoon Meeting
(a continuation)

There is no doubt that John actually understands our earthly life when he says "We ought to lay down our lives for the brethren." We need only to think of the example he sets before us, of Jesus. Of course, he does not mean in the same way that military servicemen are obligated to sacrifice their lives on the battlefield for their country

---

* No doubt reference is made here to the seven-year, legally-enforced separation of the author and his wife because their marriage was not performed in the state church. (See Introduction to Volume I.)

(as one says), and yet it is a war, a *battle* and a *struggle* that is appointed to the disciples of Christ in this world, in which they are indebted to lay down their lives, since, for Christ's sake, they are considered as sheep for the slaughter. And just as soldiers need not be on the battlefield every day but still have to be prepared and ready to fight on any day, at any call, so are the true sheep of Christ also indebted to lay down their lives and are in danger of it continually (Romans 8; I Corinthians 15).

This spiritual war exists between Christ and Belial and wherever Christ enters, contention and division arises (Luke 12:49; Matthew 10),

> "I am come to send fire on the earth; and
> what will I, if it be already kindled?"

and, of course, it is still as we see in the case of Christ Himself, that through apparent outward defeat we gain the real victory over the world and the devil, by not sparing our sanctified life in order to win eternal life, since the devil aims to rob us of eternal life and the blessedness of our souls because he begrudges anyone redemption, and he who shall attain eternal life must purchase it by offering up his earthly life. But the devil cannot rob anyone of eternal life who does not have it, and by nature no one has it for the devil has already robbed all men of it in Adam; but it is given to us again in Christ. Therefore the devil again seeks to rob all those of Christ who have actually received Him as their life; from the others he cannot only not rob Christ, but they even serve the devil against Christ and His members on earth.

But if we are indebted even to lay down our lives we can conclude from this what love to the brethren obligates us to do in the case of the greater toward the lesser (verse 17):

> "But whoso hath this world's good, and
> seeth his brother have need, and shutteth up
> his bowels of compassion [heart] from him,
> how dwelleth the love of God in him?"

To be charitable, compassionate with the poor and needy
with one's earthly good, is the first requisite, the distinguishing mark and fruit of every contrite soul (Luke
3:11), as soon as one acknowledges and deplores his
hitherto unrighteous, ungodly, idolatrous, covetous life.

> "He answereth and saith unto them, He
> that hath two coats, let him impart to him
> that hath none; and he that hath meat, let
> him do likewise."

With Zacchaeus, the tree burst forth in buds when the
new life-sap of Christ raised itself in it (Luke 19:8).

> "And Zacchaeus stood, and said unto the
> Lord; Behold, Lord, the half of my goods I
> give to the poor; and if I have taken any thing
> from any man by false accusation, I restore
> him fourfold."

Then how much more shall the believer prove his new
life in Christ by being compassionate, merciful and be-
nevolent toward needy brethren if he has the means and
is able to do it. For what shall we think of one who is
untouched and unmoved to compassion by the need of
the poor? Or if he indeed feels the desire but suppresses
and stifles it out of love for his earthly good! For he who
cannot overcome himself in this least thing still loves his
own life in this world and not Christ, and does not consider himself a servant and householder who must give
account to his Lord of that which has been entrusted to
him, but holds himself as his own master and what he has
as his own property, to do with as he likes.

Chapter LXXXI

Active Love in the Children of God

April 6, 1841 (Tuesday) ; Evening Meeting
I John 3 : 17 f.

> "But whoso hath this world's good, and seeth his brother have need, and shutteth up his bowels of compassion from him, how dwelleth the love of God in him?
>
> "My little children, let us not love in word, neither in tongue; but in deed and in truth."

The apostle calls for an *active love* in the daily life of a child of God, in great things as well as in small ones. There are two sides to the complete life of the believer: the one is hidden in the Spirit and is in relation to the Lord, Who searches the heart; the other is *revealed in love* and is in relation *to the brethren.* Now, as the inner life is constituted, so is the outer one also; i.e., if we live in the Spirit for God and love Him with all our heart, then in the flesh we live for mankind (the brethren) and serve it in love. But if we do not love the brethren, then we, likewise, do not love God and where no active love is found, there we find no true faith either, for we cannot repay the Lord for what He has done for us, but we shall repay it to the brethren. And then we have a great field to work in, and what we do in this way to the brethren for the sake of the Lord, that we have done for the Lord Himself and He in turn will recompense us on that day. Actually whatever we do we do for ourselves. Whether it be good or evil it is put to our account (Proverbs 19:17; II Corinthians 9:6; Ephesians 6:5 ff.).

"He that hath pity upon the poor lendeth unto the Lord; and that which he hath given will he pay him again."

"But this I say, He which soweth sparingly shall reap also sparingly; and he which soweth bountifully shall reap also bountifully."

"Servants, be obedient to them that are your masters according to the flesh, with fear and trembling, in singleness of your heart, as unto Christ;

"Not with eyeservice, as menpleasers; but as the servants of Christ, doing the will of God from the heart;

"With good will doing service, as to the Lord, and not to men:

"Knowing that whatsoever good thing any man doeth, the same shall he receive of the Lord, whether he be bond or free."

Paul therefore says (Romans 13:8), "Owe no man any thing, but to love one another: ..."

But what is love? It is not an idle word but a *full work,* for he who loves in word, without deed, is a liar and he who loves in tongue, without works, is a hypocrite; for love is the most holy thing: it is God Himself, and we must ever be careful that we carry on no mockery and jesting with God and profane the Holiest of all with lies, falsity and craftiness. *True divine love is Christ living in us* and working through us and therefore we—if Christ is in us—ought to lay down our life for the brethren as He has given His life out of love toward us.

However, this energetic love without which nothing at all counts or has value with Christ, is lacking in many of us. Either our love has become entirely cold and has changed into apathy or it is merely an empty word without virtue or truth. But he who hallows his whole life and brings it as an offering to the Lord must necessarily do all that he does to the glory of the Lord and in relation to Him, for the outer life is but an effluence of the inner one, be it good or evil. But if Christ dwells in us by His Spirit of Promise, a mixture of sweetness and bitterness does not flow from us, but rivers of living water (John 7:39) and those, then, by no means are empty words but lovely, as they sound: they are divine love in deed and in truth.

> "(But this spake he of the Spirit, which they that believe on him should receive: for the Holy Ghost was not yet given; because that Jesus was not yet glorified.)"

April 8, 1841 (Maunday Thursday); Morning Meeting
I John 3:16 ff.

We cannot pass over these words without having received and perceived their strength and savor in us, without which all else does not help us. Two things we need unite here so that we have eternal life and are saved, but both are united in Christ and we must not separate them. The one is Christ appeared in the *flesh* and died on the cross for our sins in order that the old man might be captured, suppressed, disempowered, slain, annihilated, or Christ has died in vain. The other is Christ coming in the *Spirit* in order to set up something new in us in place of the old, or again Christ's death avails us nothing, for by His death He has only become our Substitute and Forerunner and has broken the way, that we could follow after Him and, by His footprints, step into His life.

To this end, we must be baptized into Christ's death;

i.e., be immersed, buried and planted together with Him in the likeness of His death, so that the likeness of His resurrection and of His life with the Father follows by reason of it. For Christ has died but once, for a moment, as our sin; but because He was the Son of God, death could not hold Him and, awakened by the glory of the Father, He lives in eternity.

Consequently, he who has died with Christ to sin, must also arise to a *new life* and the death of Adam has no further power over him. For as Christ would not have been the Son of God, nor would He have become our Savior and Redeemer through His death if He had remained in death and had not risen, so are we not redeemed and children of God either if sin abides in us and selfishness rules over us. For as Christ's death was but a short passing over and through into everlasting life, so must baptism (immersion into Christ's death) be for the believer the passing over from the death of Adam into the everlasting life of Christ (Romans 6).

Therefore, it is folly to confer baptism upon little children, who lack memory and understanding, because, despite it, they live in sin afterwards, which from year to year ever manifests itself in a more flagrant form, and since such baptism *without* faith is *not* an immersion into into Christ's death, Christ's life cannot go forth from it or be put on. For in the baptized one it is Christ Who must live and no longer the old man, who allows everyone to do as he pleases.

But no one belongs to Christ or has a share in His death and life who does not have His Spirit. That is why one finds so few true Christians and so little divine love, because men do not die with Christ unto sin and consequently Christ does not live in them unto righteousness, and where that has not been brought about, it is useless for John to say: 'As He laid down His life for us, so ought we to lay down our lives for the brethren.' It still does not achieve this and is an impossibility as long as the old man has not died and one, accordingly, still loves his life in the world and is fearful of losing something; for he who has died in this way no longer has anything of his *own* except *Christ* and can lose nothing any more in this world.

With reference to sin, the citation Proverbs 20:9,

> "Who can say, I have made my heart clean,
> I am pure from my sin?"

has no further application in the New Testament or, rather, anyone who has Christ must answer Solomon's question affirmatively. But he who would still refer to Solomon's claim now and comfort himself in his sin would, just by that, confess that he has not yet known, found, received or put on Christ as the redemption from sin and as the life from death. For we can see and hear what Solomon had not yet seen and heard. Thus one can know who is still under the Old Testament and who is in the New.

Chapter LXXXII
True Teachers and Preachers

April 8, 1841 (Maunday Thursday); Afternoon Meeting
I John 3:16 ff.

If Christ has attained in us the purpose of His death by the abolition of sin, then we must become His real followers and imitators in *our* life, as He *Himself* will live and walk and function in us by His work in the world, for which He has come into the flesh as the Eternal Word of God, out of which all His children become born anew. However this first manifestation of Christ always takes place in the form of a servant, by being obedient and doing the will of the Father, and we must be disposed to accommodate ourselves to it as members of His body, the church, and must dismiss all lofty ideas about ourselves.

Christ always comes into the world as the Truth, as He said to Pilate (John 18:37):

> " . . . . Thou sayest that I am a king. To this end was I born, and for this cause came I into the world, that I should bear witness unto the truth. Every one that is of the truth heareth my voice."

for nothing save it, the Word of Truth, has a redemptive and regenerative power in man. But the world does what Pilate did and most scornfully asks, "What is truth?" It does not desire to see or to hear or to tolerate the truth. It has an aversion for it, like King Ahab had for the Prophet Micah, because the truth does not speak as the world would like to have it and prophesies nothing good for it. As often as Christ comes into the world He has to suffer and be crucified again in His believers and saints, in the members of His body, and although He has died only once for sin, His Passion evermore continues until the time that He comes in glory; and by Him the thoughts of many hearts will be revealed, *pro* and *contra*.

In no other way than by His Spirit dwelling in us are we members of His body. But if Christ is in us, we must let Him use us for whatever He will; even as there is no useless member on our body (at least it should not be so for we dislike lame or usless members). Also, in no other way can Christ influence the world to persuasion and redemption than by coming in His Word and Spirit (i.e.

in His members, John 16) and bearing witness of the Truth. But just as He was not known and received as the Son of God the first time, so is He now still not known and received by the world, but rejected, blasphemed and crucified as a seducer and deceiver, and yet, just as no one is a Christian without Christ's Spirit of Life, so also no one as a teacher can preach Christ without the Spirit of Truth, which reproves the world, and for that reason all true teachers and witnesses of Christ must suffer with Him. All those who would teach without the Spirit of Christ are seducers and deceivers because no soul is saved and converted and born again by their seed as the Word of God, which is the Truth, namely Christ.

In the world however, the usual thing is as Solomon says (Proverbs 16:2):

> "All the ways of a man are clean in his own
> eyes; but the Lord weigheth the spirits."

If it were now true, that everyone by and for himself knows and walks upon the right way of salvation, there would be no need for teachers and guides of the only right way and one could just let all go the way they please and know and are accustomed to going. However if one recognizes the need for teachers and preachers, then, just by that fact, one acknowledges that men do not know the right way of life by themselves and that they must be led, and then it is a question of whether the pretentious teachers and guides of the blind are so disposed that they can show men the only true Way, i.e. Christ. And because no one is in a position to do that except him who fearlessly speaks the truth through the Spirit of Christ and, further, because all those in whom Christ dwells and testifies are hated and rejected by the world as seducers, the world is deceived by its false teachers and blind guides and it is evident that men do not know Christ as the only Way to Life, neither do they walk in Him, because they do not the will of God but the will of the flesh; and whereas, according to the Scriptures, there is only one way to salvation, in the world it is thought there are thousands of ways because to each one his own way seems right.

Now if I will teach others, then I am responsible for the word that I speak, whether or not it is Christ the Truth; and if it is Christ Who speaks through me, then all who hear the Word are responsible for it, for they could and should be redeemed and saved by the Word of Truth. But if it is not Christ in me, then I am a seducer and a deceiver as are all those who do not testify by Christ's Spirit of Truth. But if I know Christ and do not confess Him it will be required of me. Thus a follower of Christ must have the mind of Moses, that he prefers the reproach of Christ to the honor of men and willingly lets himself be regarded and treated as an offscouring and an expiatory sacrifice of the world, in anticipation of the reward.

As we, therefore, must first, in a spiritual way (in baptism), be crucified with Christ and must die according to the old man of sin, thus we still must afterwards be also crucified in our own person or body with Him and die following Him, so that in eternity we may live and reign with Him (II Timothy 2 : 8 ff.).

> "Remember that Jesus Christ of the seed
> of David was raised from the dead according
> to my gospel:
> "Wherein I suffer trouble, as an evil doer,
> even unto bonds; but the word of God is not
> bound.
> "Therefore I endure all things for the
> elect's sakes, that they may also obtain the

salvation which is in Christ Jesus with eternal glory.

"It is a faithful saying: For if we be dead with him, we shall also live with him:

"If we suffer, we shall also reign with him: . . ."

But if the former has not been brought to pass in us, we are not qualified for the latter, for where the old man has not died, there one has not risen with Christ and for that reason cannot risk his life. A learned, mechanical faith does not help us in this, only the living faith of the heart.

Chapter LXXXIII

The Firm Foundation

April 11, 1841 (Sunday) ; Morning Meeting
I John 3 : 16 ff.

"Hereby perceive we the love of God, because he laid down his life for us: and we ought to lay down our lives for the brethren.

"But whoso hath this world's good, and seeth his brother have need, and shutteth up his bowels of compassion from him, how dwelleth the love of God in him?

"My little children, let us not love in word, neither in tongue; but in deed and in truth."

Christ's death and resurrection have been fulfilled and substantiated in him whose mind, thought and endeavor is for that which is above, where Christ is, not for that which is on earth (Colossians 3) ; for where one's treasure is, there his heart is also and that to which the heart clings in love is its god. For the love of men is undividedly directed upon *one thing,* not upon two opposing things, not upon God and the world at the same time. All men indeed seek something—not God and His kingdom—but the world and what is of it and hence are never satisfied, never find rest: they cannot say, "I now have found the firm foundation." But he who has found Christ will truly be satisfied and will possess all in One.

Therefore, the kingdom of heaven is compared to a merchantman who seeks goodly, genuine pearls, as the parable goes (Matthew 13). He seeks and indeed nothing worthless, ordinary, vain, or earthly, but the veritable and the heavenly, although he himself does not yet know what it is until he has found Christ and, in Him, the real, everlasting riches. But the seeker is no longer satisfied with the things that are perishable; he strives after his real designation, after fellowship with the living God. Now, for that, God Himself has made provision and has come nigh to men in His *Son* in order to reconcile the world with Himself. But that is not yet sufficient for the union of man with God. Men on their part must also come nigh to God, in the *Son*. They must relinquish the enmity and accept the reconciliation. Therefore the proclamation of the good message is "Repent and be converted and believe on the Son for the kingdom of God is at hand."

But men do not accept God's offer of love; they remain hostile in the disposition of the flesh and strive after that which is of the world. It is true, it seems as if they were seeking God and drawing themselves nigh to Him when they appear to reverence Him outwardly, with their lips, but while they draw nigh to God with their mouth, their heart is far from Him; their thoughts are not of Him but of the world and their pretended worship of God is hypocrisy, deceit and vanity (Matthew 15). For sinners, there is no approach to God except in the Son, Who has entered midway between God and us so as to remove the partition-wall and make the union possible. And as soon as one is converted and enters into Christ, the veil is parted and he is in fellowship with the Father, for the Father and the Son are One and whoever is in the Son is also in the Father.

No one of himself, however, seeks God first, but God seeks and calls us first, and our seeking after the *veritable* (the goodly pearl) is the result thereof and the proof that He has begun to work in us, so that the *seeking* soul can all the more confidently get a footing and be certain of finding what he seeks and more than he has sought, a pearl of great price! and the proof of this discovery is that man, rejoicing, goes and sells all that he has to buy the pearl. Anyone who is really in earnest about seeking need not always seek, for each one who truly seeks, finds (Matthew 7) and then rejoices in his possession and he need seek no further on earth.

In this respect, there are but three kinds of people: (a) such who do not yet seek for the veritable but for the perishable; (b) such who really seek and are therefore certain of their finding; (c) such who have found Christ and give up everything else for Him, for the heart of man can be bound to only one place, either above in heaven or beneath on earth. For that reason his heart, whose treasure is Christ, must be in heaven and free here below, that he may not again become entangled and be captured, for he who clings to the world is still living in sin. Each of the two is inseparable—love for the world and love for sin.

April 11, 1841 (Sunday); Afternoon Meeting
(a continuation)

John requires sacrificial love for the brethren as a duty

and an obligation of the children of God because it, as the divine nature, must be implanted and be innate in them, without which they are not children of God, and the goal of love does indeed not consist in some alms or gifts and works of compassion, in which, otherwise, many of the rich would have the glory and advantage over many of the poor. But that is not the standard according to which God judges (Luke 21 : 1 ff.).

> "And he looked up, and saw the rich men casting their gifts into the treasury.
> "And he saw also a certain poor widow casting in thither two mites.
> "And he said, Of a truth I say unto you, that this poor widow hath cast in more than they all:
> "For all these have of their abundance cast in unto the offerings of God: but she of her penury hath cast in all the living that she had."

Instead, the disposition which manifests itself in the giving of one's self and the offering up of one's life for the brethren is the standard, and the children of God are obligated to it because they have vowed it in the baptism of Christ and have solemnly promised to cleave only to Him and to follow Him in the power of godliness (I Timothy 2 : 10; II Timothy 3 : 12; I Peter 3 : 21).

> "But (which becometh women professing godliness) with good works."

> "Yea, and all that will live godly in Christ Jesus shall suffer persecution."

> "The like figure whereunto even baptism doth also now save us (not the putting away

of the filth of the flesh, but the answer of a good conscience toward God,) by the resurrection of Jesus Christ:"

Every vow that is made to God is binding but it must be made voluntarily and from conviction, not thoughtlessly nor by constraint.

All believers who let themselves be baptized in Christ are then in the same position and situation as Christ was in when on earth. For, as God in the Old Testament had let it be proclaimed and promised through Moses and the prophets beforetime that in the fulness of time He would send a Redeemer out of Zion to save His people from their sins, and the Son said "Behold, I come," and He actually came when the time was fulfilled to die for our sins and to perform the will of the Father, so shall we likewise not only promise godliness but imitate Christ in deed as well and bring our lives to God as a holy, living and acceptable sacrifice. For what would have become of us if the Lord had not fulfilled His promise, and further how could His truthfulness stand if we had always waited in vain for the Promised Savior? But just as the Lord loved us not in word only, nor in tongue, but in the deed itself and in truth, thus must we love also, not with beautiful, worthless words and a lying tongue, but in deed and in truth and thereby fulfil the vow that we promised Christ in baptism.

The world does not mean or interpret it in that way with its baptism, that they had obligated themselves by it to bring their life in the world as a sacrifice to Christ, and yet all maintain that they are baptized; and they hate and rail at us because we disallow the baptism of little children. The Lord will therefore hold them responsible for it and demand of them the fruit of baptism. Both are in an equally bad situation, those who have never made the vow of baptism and those who have indeed made it but have never kept it, namely so as to lead a holy and godly life in the world in the imitation of Christ and to bring themselves as a sacrifice to God. There is nothing else that we can do to be saved but to make our promise to Christ and then keep it, for all who let themselves be baptized into Christ also receive the power to fulfil it and if they do then not do so it is their own fault.

The world wants to make things easy for itself with its counterfeit baptism, for in their craftiness they think: if the intention of baptism is that we must give up sinning and our life, then we will have nothing of it (the old kind is more lenient). But the Lord will catch them in their intrigue and they will have to confess either that they are *not* baptized or that they are damned because they have not the fruit of baptism.

It, of course, depends not upon the willing or running of men but upon the *grace of God in Christ*. However, if, under the Old Testament (the law) we already have promised a thousand times that we would lead a godly life if we were once saved from the body of this death, then we shall actually fulfil it under the New Testament (the Gospel of Grace), inasmuch as in Christ we have not only the will to do but the accomplishment, so that we may not be found liars with our promise of godliness, even though we have to suffer on account of it.

CHAPTER LXXXIV

FAITHFULNESS IN DAILY LIFE

April 16, 1841 (Friday) ; Evening Meeting
I John 3 : 17

> "But whoso hath this world's good, and
> seeth his brother have need, and shutteth up
> his bowels of compassion from him, how
> dwelleth the love of God in him?"

Faithfulness in the little things of daily life in the home circle, etc., is all the more important and necessary for the children of God so that their light may shine and their divine nature, the lovableness of Christ, be revealed *there* where we spend most of our lifetime—at home—and yet, because this is customary we are tempted there to permit neglect of the proper attention and tenderness, especially in distributing gifts of charity to needy brethren when parsimony and the timidity of unbelief generally over-reach themselves.

For if it actually requires wisdom from above to determine to whom one should give, since shameless beggars and deceivers so often misuse the name of Christ and the compassion of the believers, one would surely be able to do much more, even for poverty, than one is inclined to do in most cases to come to the distress of needy brethren whom one sees suffering, and how much more need there is which one does not see and know about! Even if we could not lay up much ourselves, divine love is always *rich* because it draws in a direct way from the Living Fountain, and faith, which gives single-heartedly, does not ask security for itself, yet never comes to shame, for God always helps him again who takes pity on and cares for those in distress, when he himself is in need (Psalm 41).

If only we would enjoy being conduits of the well of God, whose waters never fail, we would always have enough and even an abundance. And what are we *without* the love of God? Nothing but "sounding brass or a tinkling cymbal"! Now, if our heart is locked up when it comes to sharing what we have with others, then God Himself is locked out and blessedness is too, for the love of God alone makes us ourselves and others blessed.

Chapter LXXXV

"In Deed and In Truth"

April 18, 1841 (Sunday); Morning Meeting
I John 3 : 18 ff.

"My little children, let us not love in word,
neither in tongue; but in deed and in truth.
"And hereby we know that we are of the
truth, and shall assure our hearts before him.
"For if our heart condemn us, God is greater than our heart, and knoweth all things."

"We ought to lay down our lives for the brethren." By that, John does not mean only some but *all the baptized*, who have promised godliness, not an appearance of godliness but its power, so as to follow Christ by His footsteps since He has laid down His soul (His life) for us. Whoever does not thus take to heart his baptism does not know what baptism is or why he allowed himself to be baptized into Christ's death. This is still much more the case with those who were baptized as unknowing children and who, later as adults, in no instance, would have allowed themselves to be baptized had they understood what baptism signifies so that it might be the appeal [testimony] of a *good conscience* to God and not an external work. For no one can be baptized without his own conviction and consent, and faith of heart and confession of mouth.

But to establish the proof of a good conscience, the vow of baptism must be kept, inviolably, and here we come to a fine and difficult point which does not concern those who are not in earnest about a holy, godly life in Christ Jesus; namely, since John says: "And hereby we know that we are of the truth, ... For if our heart condemn us, God is greater than our heart," etc. Of this inner witnessing, censuring, punishing, accusing and disciplining, no carnal man knows anything, for the world cannot receive the Spirit of Truth, and in its place has made of the grace of God, a broad highway of every kind of sin and vice, upon which the profligate and impenitent are pronounced righteous, whereas the *true grace of God* is first a *saving* and then a *disciplining* (an instructing) grace.

But its discipline and instruction is another than that of the law, for Moses has a visible office, in tables of stone, and is a visible schoolmaster who handles each transgression with corporal punishment and correction. To him the disobedient, bad boys who will not leave the mischievousness and malice of their hearts, go to school and although he at once breaks his rod in pieces upon them (Exodus 32), yet with all his zeal he accomplishes nothing. He therefore has a difficult office and a hard life and is a troubled man (Numbers 12:3).

> "(Now the man Moses was very meek, above all the men which were upon the face of the earth.)"

Not until we have recognized the purpose of the law and *at the same time* that of the death of Christ and with contrite hearts have *believed* so as to die with Christ unto the old man and to renounce the service of the devil, can we advance to the higher school where the Holy Ghost teaches and disciplines us *inwardly,* that we may become instructed in heavenly things and the mysteries of the kingdom of heaven by Him, as real children of God, whereas Moses teaches only earthly things.

But the Holy Ghost is such a pure, gentle Teacher and Instructor of the children of God that they must obey His merest beckoning so as not to grieve Him. His discipline is hidden within, and a pure, tranquil heart is necessary to hear Him. He dislikes to contend with us if we are wont to be unruly and vexatious; and if we grieve Him by continual unfaithfulness and disobedience He will eventually forsake us as He forsook the first world (Genesis 6), to our own will and perdition, and then the apostatized can sin and be carnally- and worldly-minded and no longer feel it because they no longer have any disciplining whatever, neither by the law nor by grace. From here things go down grade without a stop being put to them and men *twice* become dead trees (Hebrews 6 and 10).

April 18, 1841 (Sunday); Afternoon Meeting

As reborn, pardoned children of God, we must love in truth, not hypocritically or deceitfully with false, feigned words. Real divine love does not make much ado and many words but proves itself by the very deed; it does not promise much and fulfil little but does more than one, according to human standards, can demand of the world, namely the giving up of one's self and the sacrificing of one's life for the brethren, in that real divine love, as a power of godliness, continues onward in the footsteps of Christ. For where the Holy Spirit of Truth dwells in man as a living law, there He outdoes and overrules the human and the sentient in man which, otherwise, obstructingly and disturbingly step in the way.

Neither does it suffice for the edification of the church if only one or a few sacrifice themselves, but every single one of the church must show the same diligence and zeal (Hebrews 6) for on the body of Christ there are no idle, unnecessary, let alone harmful, members (John 15). Whence then are they? Certainly not from Christ (II Corinthians 11; Matthew 13), and one unsound member does more harm in the church than ten or twenty zealous ones can do for the good. Therefore there must be a working together of all in the one Spirit of Christ, in which no one seeks his own but each one that which is Christ's and the brethren's.

Now where the Spirit of Christ has become powerful over the flesh, there the love of God is in effect and has no other law over it but is itself the highest (commandment) law, which teaches the good, acceptable and perfect will of God (Romans 12). "Hereby we know that we are of the truth," i.e., of Christ, begotten and born of the seed of God (James 1; I Peter 1), not as a perishable flower, but as an everlasting fruit of God and the firstlings of His creatures.

If however a child of God—one who is not slow to good works, not indifferent toward evil, but constantly zealous for God and lives faithfully according to the rule of the Spirit—should, for all that, slip back and deviate in some way from this holy rule (even though unrevealed) and accordingly grieves instead of pleases the Holy Spirit, the inner punishment of the Spirit follows immediately thereupon, as thunder upon lightning, and although this for a moment disturbs our inner peace, yet it is so far from putting an end to our state of grace that John rather declares this inner judgment and testimony of the Spirit to be a definite sign that we are of the truth, for an unconverted, unbelieving person knows and experiences nothing of this inner Schoolmaster, not even in grievous sins, which a child of God would not at all allow himself (Ephesians 4 and 5).

However, a child of God must at once turn to the Father with a confession of His transgression as soon as the lightning of the sin has flashed through his soul and the voice of God has followed upon it, so that it may be forgiven and may not be recorded in the book of remembrance. Then after the thunder and lightning, a salutary rain usually bursts in a flood of tears, as in Peter's case (Matthew 26). But we shall not think that we are permitted to apply the blood of Christ for such sins, which was not shed for sins after the pardoning but for those only of the time of ignorance; for *sins unto death, after one's pardoning,* are not forgiven any more because Christ will not die again. But he who would know what is the inner judgment of the Spirit must himself go into the sanctuary of God. For the unconsecrated, nothing more can be said of this; one can merely point it out to them as an incentive.

April 20, 1841 (Tuesday); Evening Meeting
I John 3 : 19 ff.

> "And hereby we know that we are of the truth, and shall assure our hearts before him.
> "For if our heart condemn us, God is greater than our heart, and knoweth all things.
> "Beloved, if our heart condemn us not, then have we confidence toward God.

"And whatsoever we ask, we receive of him, because we keep his commandments, and do those things that are pleasing in his sight."

The first requisite and condition is that we be of the truth, i.e., be born of God, that Christ may be in us by the *Spirit of Truth;* no longer the lying spirit of the world (the devil) as by nature is the case with all men, who, for that reason, know and understand nothing of the light and testimony that the children of God have in them, by which they instantly recognize and stifle each deviation (inclination to, and allurement of, sin) in the bud, so that it may not come to the deed or fruit and the field of their heart be not grown over with thorns and thistles and the kingdom of God choked up in them (Hebrews 6).

That a child of God may not sin, therefore depends upon his faithfulness toward the inner guidance and discipline of the Holy Ghost, for if a man of God does not desire to sin, it is not necessary for him to do so and if he should sin, then he must do so voluntarily, in that he, knowingly and with lust, gives place to the hidden inclination of sin and indulges in it and consequently is unfaithful to the Spirit of Grace. It is a comfort for the faithful that they, with anxious care, are fearful of backsliding and apostasy for just this fear of God protects them from the fall.

Indeed the Spirit of Truth, as the Representative of Christ, has a punitive office also for the world (John 16) and reproves the unconverted of sin so that they may come from the lie to the truth. But only those who are *reborn* of the Word of Truth have the Spirit of Truth *dwelling in them* as their Teacher, Guide and Instructor in the way of righteousness and indeed in a more perfect way than Jesus Himself by His personal appearance could prepare for His disciples. However, because the Holy Spirit is the last and greatest gift of God which man can receive here below, the greatest faithfulness and attention to His hidden voice and wink accordingly is required of those who have received Him so that He may be able to lead them *with His eyes* into all truth, just as good children obey their parents upon a mere look (without punishment) so as not to grieve, but please, their hearts.

And because we are not children of God unless we have died to sin and have received a new, pure, willing heart conformable to Christ's, we must become accustomed to obeying the gentle and tender guidance of the Holy Spirit at its slightest beckoning so that we may avoid every sin. And since God gives His *last* and *supernal* gift to none but those who have been born anew by the Word of Truth, the loss of the same (by wilful apostasy and disobedience) is irreparable and he who then dies again cannot be quickened a second time for such have crucified Christ afresh unto themselves.

For this reason, the Lord has commanded an outward discipline as well, in addition to the inward one of the Spirit, which He either administers in a direct way Himself (I Corinthians 11) or lets be executed through the church, by reproof and discipline (I Corinthians 3 and 5), namely if a believer forgets himself to the extent that he falls in open sins. But he has erred if he has so neglected the inner discipline of the Spirit that he must be punished outwardly, and it is very much to be feared and has been proved by precedent that such unfaithfulness hardly ever regains the right soundness of health in the Spirit because the real children of God are called to do all that they do, in the name of Jesus and to the glory of God as long as they live in the world.

CHAPTER LXXXVI

THE DOUBLE DISTINGUISHING MARK

April 23, 1841 (Friday); Evening Meeting
I John 3 : 19 ff.

> "And hereby we know that we are of the truth, and shall assure our hearts before him.
> "For if our heart condemn us, God is greater than our heart, and knoweth all things.
> "Beloved, if our heart condemn us not, then have we confidence toward God."

The apostle gives us a double distinguishing mark by which we may know that we are of the truth and have the spiritual life of Christ in us. First the negative: if our heart condemns us for every unfaithfulness to the holy rule and every deviation from it. Of course, not every deviation is one from the truth, but the inner censuring and punishing on account of it is a proof and testimony that the truth of Christ dwells in the man and that the heart of this man is pledged to the truth and, as a rule, watches sternly over and is zealous for its purity.

Such deviation in a child of God is the exception only and not a matter of habit. Yet these exceptions must always become fewer the more faithfully one follows the Spirit of Christ because a child of God dislikes being disciplined and prefers to have peace with the Father and joy in the Holy Ghost; and just as the sea will suffer nothing dead in it but casts it up, so the pure Spirit of Christ will likewise suffer no impurity in the heart. Where one gives room to the impure spirit, there the pure Spirit of Truth must depart, for He does not in vain punish and discipline each sinful impulse, but so that the man of

God may be purified of every sin and may lead a holy life in the world.

It is for this very reason that the inner judgment is a sign of the truth and spiritual health of one, for men of the world know nothing of it. They treat all kinds of sinning with indifference and if they should perhaps still hear a condemning voice in their conscience (how else does God keep a door open for Himself even in the conscience of natural man? Romans 2:15),

> "Which shew the work of the law written
> in their hearts, their conscience also bearing
> witness, and their thoughts the mean while
> accusing or else excusing one another;)"

they are not inclined to hearken to this warning and punishment, but stifle the voice of their screaming conscience and bring it to silence and excuse and justify themselves in regard to their sins. Even if the spoken word of reproof is added to it, they will have nothing held against them. But the children of God, who are of the truth, are not so; they accuse and bewail themselves before God of each transgression so that it may be forgiven them; they do not wish to conceal anything for it is God Who enlightens them and Who knows all things. For as soon as one is converted, the inner judgment comes into power and action and if one walks *faithfully* after that, he is free from the punitive correction of the heart and is also anxious to *keep* himself free from it; however, not like the unconverted, by the denial of sin, but by the denial of all that is ungodly and the worldly lusts. That is the difference between the children of God and the children of the devil.

Hypocrites also know very well what is right or not right and they see it too and judge and censure every sin, only not in themselves but in others. Indeed, they judge and blame the children of God for that too which, in itself, is not even sin but a weakness—so holy a life do they demand of the children of God! But those who *are* of the truth, above all direct their critical eye at themselves and not at others and by virtue of this severity toward themselves, they may then on an occasion of over-hastiness, appeal to God and assure (quiet and assuage) their hearts before Him without becoming self-deceiving hypocrites and liars, for God is omniscient, knowing not only their deviation but also their remorse, pain, self-accusation.

April 25, 1841 (Sunday) ; Morning Meeting
I John 3 : 19 ff.

It is toward God that we stand in the highest and most important relationship of our life inasmuch as He is the Judge of all the world. Therefore we must enter into the closest fellowship and circle of acquaintance with Him, that we may know how we stand with Him and come not into judgment. The world does not know the living God, feels no drawing to Him, and, accordingly, does not understand sin. On the other hand, all children of God know their Father and have an open and a joyous access to Him, which they will not again allow to be closed to them by sin. Therefore they guard themselves against sin so that they may not lose the peace of God.

Now when John speaks of a condemning or an accusing of the heart, he does not mean it of the beginning of a sinner's conversion, when the judgment of damnation for the time of ignorance thunders so loudly and terribly in the heart that the frightened sinner ventures not so much as to lift up his eyes to God but smites his breast, much less then could he threaten the storm and still the tempest himself. Then nothing except the voice of Christ can help us, which brings rest to the soul (Matthew 11:28)

> "Come unto me, all ye that labor and are
> heavy laden, and I will give you rest."

and indeed so wondrously and quickly that man must kneel down and worship and acknowledge that He is the Lord, and after this greatest experience of His power and glory, the pardoned one never again doubts that the same Lord Jesus has the power to defy every tempest and to rescue him from every danger, anxiety and temptation. For there is no tempest as great and as terrible as sin, and when the heart has once become free, peaceful and quieted of sin, it is also armed against every outward storm of the enemy, without being thrown into confusion or removed from composure.

But John speaks here of the children of God, who are already of the truth, that they possess and have in control their own heart and so can quiet it before God their Father, without deceiving or wrongly comforting or absolving themselves as does the unbelieving world, which forgives its own sins instead of seeking forgiveness from God and converting themselves from sin to Him, and while the hypocrites slander the Son of God, saying that He forgives sins which alone is the province of God, these same hypocrites are not afraid of absolving themselves.

The children of God however can quiet their hearts before God because they are upright before Him and, like the Father, hate all that is sin, and because they hate sin, they avoid it and therefore they are differentiated from those who are still under the law but in original conversion and who indeed hate sin too, but still commit it because they have not yet put on Christ (Romans

7). For those things about which a child of God is still condemned in his heart are not the gross, grievous sins against the old law, but are such things apart from them that, as well, are unbecoming of saints, who are severe and exact with themselves and who give account to God for every unnecessary word and impure thought.

Of such severe judgment of one's self, the world knows and understands little, if anything, and the ungodly for that reason slander the children of God as fools, saying that they have scruples about little things and will no longer have fellowship with the unfruitful works of darkness but rather reprove them: for sin is the greatest misfortune that can happen to a person, worse than breaking one's neck and limbs (Matthew 5:29).

> "And if thy right eye offend thee, pluck it out, and cast it from thee: for it is profitable for thee that one of thy members should perish, and not that thy whole body should be cast into hell."

And because every sin is first embryonic and must be present in thought and desire before it comes to the deed, all children of God must watch over their heart and guard it.

April 25, 1841 (Sunday); Afternoon Meeting
(a continuation)

John obviously wishes to comfort the children of God when he says "God is greater than our heart," — the Father is greater than the children. Our heart can accuse and condemn us, but God is a righteous Judge Who acquits His children (Romans 8:26) because they are upright, sincere, loyal and simple-hearted concerning Him and wish to conceal nothing from Him for they know that He knows all things.

> "Likewise the Spirit also helpeth our in-
> firmities: for we know not what we should
> pray for as we ought: but the Spirit itself
> maketh intercession for us with groanings
> which cannot be uttered."

But now since we, as children of God, shall sin no more at all, it certainly is a comfort for us to know that God is greater than our heart and that He forgives our mistakes; otherwise we could despair over every deviation. But now the Father knows them, and He is known of them, and because the Spirit dwells in them, they are in direct association with the Father Himself, like the Son, in Whose name they have access to the Father and His throne of grace, and with joy and confidence and openness to the fullest extent make all their requests known to Him. The Father Himself loves them because they love the Son. They sin not maliciously or wilfully, counting on the grace of God, but err from weakness and in overhaste, for he who continually errs in the *same* sin without ever becoming healed of it has never yet sought and received the forgiveness of the same.

Children of God, as a rule, work righteousness and therefore rest for their soul and peace of heart with God is their *usual situation*. Because their heart does not accuse them of unfaithfulness, their constant association and communion with God is so distinctly perceptible and effectual that they easily and positively observe His working in them, without deceiving themselves about whether their heart has peace or not. And because they do not comfort or absolve themselves in regard to any unfaithfulness but receive their justification from God, their peace is all the less subjected to deception or assumed by it, for the Spirit of Christ enlightens them and with His unutterable groanings represents them before the Father Who, also without words, understands them because He searches the heart and knows what the mind of the spirit is in them.

Upon these conditions of peace with God depends also the reality of every prayer, that the children of God make no *vain requests* for they pray through the Spirit of the Son, not to a stone or wooden idol, but to the Living God Who knows all things and before Whom they are upright, even to the innermost foundation of their heart. Only when Christ's Spirit is in us (John 16) can we pray in the name of the Son, and since even natural earthly fathers who are yet evil, know how to give good gifts to their petitioning children (not stones for bread), the Heavenly Father would far better know how to give His petitioning children what they ask of Him in the name of the Son, so that their joy may be full. But where the heart is not pure and is not at peace with God, there the joy of drawing nigh and praying to Him is a nonentity.

Chapter LXXXVII

The Accurate Barometer of a Spiritual Life

April 27, 1841 (Tuesday) ; Evening Meeting
I John 3 : 19 ff.

All who are born of God have a continuous association with their Father and because the one true God is a living God—a Spirit Who searches, fills and knows all things— He, accordingly, gives His children His living testimony through His Holy Spirit of Truth, Who leads them in all truth. And as He teaches them so it is, verily, and not a lie, and if they follow His hidden guidance single- heartedly and faithfully, they at all times recognize the condition of their hearts rightly, without being mistaken about it.

If the Spirit condemns, disciplines and smites them inwardly, His testimony is true and they may be sure that something is wrong with them or some wrong has been done by them that must be put away, and if He does not condemn them, they may also be sure that they have peace and comfort and joy from God. And if their unremitting desire, prayer and sighing to God is "Teach me to live according to Thy good pleasure for Thou art my God. May thy good Spirit lead me on the *straight path*," they may be assured that their prayers will be granted and that the Father will not permit them to be given over to the lying and erring spirit for, above all, it is always the will of God that we do the good and never the evil because He loves only righteousness and hates ungodliness. And if the children of God use the ability rightly that is given to them and follow the drawing and impelling powers of the Holy Ghost, they will never sin or violate their peace.

The Father has therefore placed an absolutely accurate barometer in their hearts, by which they can without fail observe the atmospheric conditions of their spiritual life and keep themselves informed of them. Indeed, if they are very faithful, attentive and obedient, their barometer becomes so sensitive that every change is indicated in advance, that they may stand guard over and conduct themselves accordingly, and the more faithful they are, the more certain they may be that they can depend upon it. But as a barometer that is out of order no longer indicates changes in the weather, so also an unfaithful, an unsettled, indifferent, inconstant, a devious and distracted heart is no longer sensitive to every change that takes place in it. Then one can sin without noticing it and without being condemned because of it, and although it is not a good thing if we must be punished and smitten, yet it is still better if we are disciplined over each deviation and errancy than if we are insensitive and without feeling with regard to them.

Therefore, as a rule the inner condition of a child of God will be one of peace and joy in God. But if it is sorrow and sadness, we should be careful to observe whether it is a spiritual and godly, or a carnal and worldly sorrow, for godly sorrow works salvation and life but worldly sorrow death and destruction (II Corinthians 7). And though we should be robbed of every earthly comfort, we must nevertheless not abandon ourselves to the sorrow of the world but think it is the will of Him, without which not even a hair can fall from our head (Matthew 28:18),

> "And Jesus came and spake unto them, saying, All power is given unto me in heaven and in earth."

much less anything else befall us that is greater and more important than a hair of our head. But if our sorrow is a godly one, it is either because of our *own unfaithfulness* or the sad condition of *others*, which we, as living members of the body of Christ, also feel and bear (I Corinthians 12:26),

> "And whether one member suffer, all the members suffer with it; or one member be honoured, all the members rejoice with it."

as did Paul, who testifies that he had great heaviness and continual sorrow in his heart for his erring brethren according to the flesh (Romans 9:1 ff.).

> "I say the truth in Christ, I lie not, my conscience also bearing me witness in the Holy Ghost,

"That I have great heaviness and continual sorrow in my heart.

"For I could wish that myself were accursed from Christ for my brethren, my kinsmen according to the flesh:

"Who are Israelites; to whom pertaineth the adoption, and the glory, and the covenants, and the giving of the law, and the service of God, and the promises;

"Whose are the fathers, and of whom as concerning the flesh Christ came, who is over all, God blessed for ever. Amen."

For if we ourselves are saved, we are not indifferent about others being lost and whoever does not concern himself about the salvation of others does not really work out his own salvation.

April 30, 1841 (Friday); Evening Meeting
I John 3 : 19 ff.

If the word "God is greater than our heart," shall be a word of comfort, it presupposes a true heart with fine feelings that does not trifle with sin but is saddened, troubled, anxiously concerned and contrite over each instance of deviation, that it may not fall into despair and out of its peaceful composure and stronghold. For the devil not only lies in wait for our souls that he—either by high-mindedness, boldness and pride or by faint-heartedness and despair—may take advantage of us, but our heart also is equally inclined to both extremes (extremes touch each other) and the sudden transition from pride to despair is unavoidable in all who have not the living God (as we see this of Judas), and pride ever comes before the fall.

But a faithful child of God, by watching and praying

continually, is kept from both extremes. Yet we shall not think that we have been snatched away from all danger and are not susceptible to temptation, or that we have already graduated from the school of God, lest this conceit in itself would already be the nearest way to the fall. That is why the apostles warn so often against our own worldly wisdom, foolish imagination, presumptuousness, etc. (Romans 12; I Corinthians 10) and exhort us to humility and lowliness of heart (I Peter 5 : 5 ff.).

> "Likewise, ye younger, submit yourselves unto the elder. Yea, all of you be subject one to another, and be clothed with humility: for God resisteth the proud, and giveth grace to the humble.
>
> "Humble yourselves therefore under the mighty hand of God, that he may exalt you in due time:
>
> "Casting all your care upon him; for he careth for you.
>
> "Be sober, be vigilant; because your adversary the devil, as a roaring lion, walketh about, seeking whom he may devour:
>
> "Whom resist stedfast in the faith, knowing that the same afflictions are accomplished in your brethren that are in the world."

If such exhortations and inferences drawn from observation were not necessary, they would not have been given to the saints; for as the law speaks to *those* who are in the *law* and does not declare itself to those who are *without* the law (Romans 3), so also does the Gospel speak to those only who are in grace and not to the unconverted. If we stand we shall see to it that we do not fall.

Midway between the two extremes of pride and despair is the right humility of heart which guards against both and a humble man is always aware that he himself is nothing and God is All and alone great and exalted. Here the word that *God is greater than we are* is the right talisman of preservation and even though our heart should condemn us of a deviation, without self-deception of any kind it can by conviction quiet and assure itself that God is greater than our heart.

For as David (Psalm 51) according to the manner and the conditions of the Old Testament comforted himself in his great twofold sin by this, that God would not cast him away from His presence and, instead of every other sacrifice, offered a contrite heart and an anxious spirit and actually found grace because of his uprightness (although he was punished for it in his temporal life), so may a child of God in the New Testament also, according to the measure of transgression appeal to His Heavenly Father without being either overbearing in boldness or swallowed up by despair (although a pardoned one in the New Testament could become guilty of no such sin as David's without dying for it, because *here* the grace received in the new life after the forgiveness of the former sins is greater than *there*).

For he who is unmindful that God is greater than his heart sets himself not *under* but *against* God, exalts himself above Him and becomes His enemy in the disposition of the flesh, and he who at all times continues to be unmindful that *God is greater* than he himself is, is a fool and falls from one sin into another (Psalm 14; Proverbs 28:26).

> "He that trusteth in his own heart is a fool: but whoso walketh wisely, he shall be delivered."

But in humble submission to God and dependence upon

Him we are comforted, joyful, full of confidence and trust, firm and strong against the adversary and secure from falling because God gives grace to the humble and the enemy must take flight.

Chapter LXXXVIII

Singleness of Heart

May 2, 1841 (Sunday) ; Morning Meeting
I John 3 : 19 ff.

John would neither comfort the indiscreet sinner who makes little of sin, nor defend sin itself, when he says: "God is greater than our heart, and knoweth all things." Instead, John reassures the upright, who take sin in an exact manner, as God takes it, for just in the greatness and omniscience of God lies the strongest reason why we should take sin rigorously and not consider it lightly, and that the Lord takes the sins of the believers rigorously is seen by the seven open letters of The Revelation, in which He says not only, "I know thy works," but, with all the praise, vindictively and reprimandly adds, "Nevertheless I have somewhat against thee," etc.; and indeed even though it were only "somewhat," He still does not allow it to be unforeboding, so that all the churches should fear and know that He tries the heart and reins. Therefore He also lays the sin of individual members as a charge to the church itself, so that the churches should prove their earnestness and strictness by the punishment and separation of the sinner; if not, He will punish without sparing the churches themselves. But if God deals thus uncompromisingly with whole churches, how much more with each individual heart!

That is exactly why Paul asks (Romans 6), "Shall we continue in sin, that grace may abound?" May we sin because of grace? And answers: "God forbid. How shall we, that are dead to sin, live any longer therein?" If we do not thus know God, that *He tries the heart and reins* and *inwardly* sets us in the light, that we may also learn to know ourselves as He knows us, then we do not know the true, living God and are lost with the world. And what does it avail us that God indeed knows us but we do not know ourselves? God looks at the heart, i.e., at the general and entire situation of one as a whole, whether one directs himself toward Him so as to please Him, and in that case will overlook a single instance of unfaithfulness about which one has sorrowed and for which one has reproved himself.

But he who would sin without taking the punishment into consideration and would merely commit more deviations (Isaiah 1:5),

> "Why should ye be stricken any more? ye
> will revolt more and more: the whole head
> is sick and the whole heart faint."

from him the Spirit of grace which otherwise dwells and testifies in the children of God (Romans 8; John 14) would also turn away. But in this it can indeed be seen whether the living God has found entry in man: if each little deviation is punished and made known. And by this we know that we have entered into the relation of sonship to the living God: if in the name of the Son we have received the right, liberty and joy to call upon Him as a Father through the Holy Ghost, to talk to Him in singleness of heart and to tell Him openly all that lies upon our heart.

But what a great, miraculous change must have taken

place in a person who in former time was an ungodly sinner and now is in a position to talk so trustingly and confidingly with the great Almighty God, as a child with his father, and to associate with Him as one friend associates with another as his equal! For when a person of lower origin or station should merely speak with one of higher rank, he feels himself impeded and restrained so that he cannot do so as freely as with his equal. And who is even an earthly king in comparison to the Lord of Heaven and Earth!

There is surely no relation as close and as heartfelt as that of a child to his father, for although the father is greater than the child, the child nevertheless is not afraid to tell him everything, unless he has a bad conscience and cannot freely and joyfully face his father, or if he is bold he will even tell lies. Thus too are many people bold toward God, in that they, for appearance's sake, would even talk (pray) to God (as for instance the pastors of the world), although they do not rightfully do so and all such prayers are nothing more than lies and an abomination before God because they do not come from the heart.

However, the more we mature as children of God, the better we also learn to know the Father in His perfection and, for this, He sends the Spirit of His Son into our hearts as a Teacher and Tutor of the future revelation of the children of God in glory and perfection, for now we are still little children compared to our great God; our knowing (judging), our prophesying, etc., now are only in part, but eventually we shall know and be known perfectly.

May 2, 1841 (Sunday); Afternoon Meeting
I John 3 : 19 ff.

> "And hereby we know that we are of the truth, and shall assure our hearts before him.
>
> "For if our heart condemn us, God is greater than our heart, and knoweth all things.
>
> "Beloved, if our heart condemn us not, then have we confidence toward God.
>
> "And whatsoever we ask, we receive of him, because we keep his commandments, and do those things that are pleasing in his sight."

The covenant of the grace of God with the man in Christ is an eternally indissoluble covenant (like the marriage bond in the temporal life) and is not dissolved if man does not want it to be (as marriage is by adultery), and since natural man is outside of this union with God because of sin (Isaiah 59:1 f.), therefore *only by sin* can the covenant of grace be dissolved again.

> "Behold, the Lord's hand is not shortened, that it cannot save; neither his ear heavy, that it cannot hear:
>
> "But your iniquities have separated between you and your God, and your sins have hid his face from you, that he will not hear."

But God on His part is so faithful in His covenant that He disciplines and chastises His children for every little defilement, so that they deny themselves of all that is ungodly and the worldly lusts and live chastely, righteously and godly in this present world. A child of God therefore is and feels himself constantly drawn to God, His Father, and if man on his part is faithful, his state of mind in the Spirit is nothing but blessedness, peace and joy, in spite of all the outward affliction and self-denial. But if he is not faithful, his state of mind insofar as he is so, is a condemning one, but the covenant is not yet dissolved by that: *the pardoned one always feels the living*

God at work in him. However, the blessed awareness of fellowship with God, the joyous drawing nigh to Him, the open-hearted communing with the Father depends upon the condition that our heart does *not* condemn us, i.e., that we keep His commandments and do what is pleasing in His sight.

Man enters into this everlasting covenant with God by holy baptism and thereupon follows the open-hearted drawing nigh to the throne of grace and the childlike appeal of the heart to the Father, in the confidence of faith that He *hears* what we ask of Him in the name of Jesus. The infallible proof that we know the living God and have fellowship with Him is this: if we utter not words to the wind or ask in vain, for if God has first called us and we have answered Him, we will call upon Him again and He will answer us. That is the test that our theory is right, for if we call upon God and ask and yet receive not what we have prayed for, it is either not the living God upon Whom we have called but an idol of our fancy (Baal, I Kings 19), or something stands in our way, because of which we are not being heard and which should first be removed, for we know that God does not hear sinners, but if anyone fears God and does righteousness he is acceptable to Him (John 9; Matthew 5; James 4).

May 4, 1841 (Tuesday); Evening Meeting
I John 3 : 20 ff.

I could not write down the extracts of the sermon. I spoke of fellowship with God as the real designation of man for blessedness in this and the future world and from which all men, because of sin and the disposition of the flesh (which is man's death), have been displaced, in that their spirit by its tendency toward vanity, is dead for God and wretched in this time and in eternity.

Chapter LXXXIX

"Evil Communications"

May 7, 1841 (Friday) ; Evening Meeting
I John 3 : 21 ff.

"If our heart condemn us not, . . . " That is the condition under which we have confidence toward God and this—whether we have confidence or not—depends upon us and our conduct toward God, for obedience to God's commandments is possible with us if we have been born of God, as then it is no longer the man himself that lives but it is Christ in him, and Christ cannot only live holy and without sin, but He cannot live otherwise at all because He cannot sin. Here some cry: "Oh well, we are not perfect like Christ. No one can live as He lived." (So said Hummel of Brugg.) Others again: "True enough Christ in us cannot sin but *we* still sin as always."

None of these know what they are saying because they know Christ not by actual experience but only after the manner of a scholar, by hearsay, and make a model of Him and pass a wrong judgment upon something they do not know and their judgment therefore can have not only no merit for us, but we must be careful to take every precaution to guard against such evil conversation, that we do not likewise become infected and corrupted by it. Against such babblers, the Apostle Paul (I Corinthians 15:33 f.) says:

> "Be not deceived: evil communications corrupt good manners.
> "Awake to righteousness, and sin not; for some have not the knowledge of God: I speak this to your shame."

Yet these think they know God and still sin and 'the truth is not in them (I John 2:3).'

> "And hereby we do know that we know him, if we keep his commandments."

Then the Word of God may say what it will, they do not believe it and make it a lie, and these are some who even consider themselves believers, and by their evil conversation become a cliff upon which many suffer shipwreck, since the heart of man is always more inclined to the lie than to the truth. But just as the devil dwells in natural man and does evil works, so Christ dwells in the reborn man and does good works and where Christ is, there the devil, the old man, is no longer to be found, for since Christ first died and then arose, He will therefore not become alive in us either unless the old man has first been crucified and has died with Him.

Then these uninformed believers ask: "Do you really not sin any more? Or isn't the old man still in you if you should still sin?" and thus give one to understand that they do not know the truth. For most certainly the old man is no longer in him who is born of God, for where the old man still lives, there man must sin (as under the law) and is not free, whether he wishes to sin or not. But where the new man (Christ) lives, man is free, so that it is not necessary for him to sin if he does not wish to (he is not a debtor to the flesh) and if he, perchance, still sins, it is not the old man who sins but he himself sins *voluntarily* because he does not watch over himself sufficiently to keep himself undefiled, for when Paul says, "The life which I now live in the flesh I live by the faith of the Son of God," he means not the flesh of sin but his earthly body.

And with such voluntary sinning, it then depends upon

whether the sins are or are not unto death, so that they either may be forgiven or may not be forgiven (Hebrews 10; II Peter 2). But if our heart does not condemn us, either we do not sin or we are deceived hypocrites if we sin and can still be at ease in spite of it.

May 9, 1841 (Sunday); Morning Meeting
I John 3:21 ff.

A person is either godly or he is ungodly; either he has the living God or he does not have Him: in him who has Him, He Himself accomplishes all that is good, all His will, for to be able to prove what is the good, acceptable and perfect will of God, man must first have known the living God Himself; i.e., he must not conform to this world but must be changed by the renewing of his mind (Romans 12).

There is indeed also an inanimate knowledge of God and His will, but it does not quicken man to do His will and to apply it to his entire life, in all that he does and says and thinks, and to examine himself and ask, "Is this pleasing to God?" For the mind of a child of God is at all times directed toward God and he does all things in relation to Him. But an ungodly man does not inquire about God and understands nothing of that which is of the Spirit of God: it is foolishness to him; and joy in God is necessary, the secret intimacy of an association with Him in particular.

Each person has his own situation to create, what he shall have and how he shall fare. If one would like to have the confidence that all that happens to him is the definite will of God and that nothing else could happen to him, he needs but to walk godly and at all times do the will of God. His lot here is in his own hands: if he does the good, it will go well with him. Then tribulation is a good thing too, that one must thank God for it. Even though men intend evil by it, God still means it well. *Godliness* is the key: all things must work together for the good and nothing can harm. Just so, the ungodly bring their misfortune upon themselves because they do the evil.

In order to be brothers and sisters of Jesus Christ, we must be *children of God*, who *do* the will of the Father and not merely *know* it. The right childship relation expresses itself in the confidence one has toward God to ask of Him all that one would have or that one lacks, and this confidence is based upon keeping His commandments and upon doing that which is acceptable to Him, and herein all children of God on earth conform to the Son (John 8:28).

> "Then said Jesus unto them, When ye have lifted up the Son of man, then shall ye know that I am he, and that I do nothing of myself; but as my Father hath taught me, I speak these things."

He does not leave them alone. He is with them and in them. Otherwise they could do nothing (good), for they are not more or greater than was the Son on earth and if *He* could do nothing of Himself but only what He had learned and heard of the Father, how should we be able to do anything of ourselves that would be pleasing to God?

All children of God—in spirit, mind and walk—bear in them the likeness of Jesus Christ the Only Begotten Son of God. They resemble Him like children of one father, for, by His incarnation the Only Begotten Son has become the *Firstborn* among *many* brethren, that He might bring *many* sons to glory. One can recognize all children of God by this spiritual physiognomy, that they do righteousness and love the brethren; just as one, on the other hand, can recognize all children of the devil by their spiritual type of face, that they commit *sin* and *hate* one another. An ever so endless diversity of features can be found in individual people by which one can distinguish them from others, and as much as the ungodly and the hypocrites may disguise and veil themselves with visible honorableness, one still recognizes them, that they are not of God.

Chapter XC

Our Designation of God

May 9, 1841 (Sunday); Afternoon Meeting
I John 3 : 21 ff.

"Beloved, if our heart condemn us not, then have we confidence toward God.

"And whatsoever we ask, we receive of him, because we keep his commandments, and do those things that are pleasing in his sight.

"And this is his commandment, That we should believe on the name of his Son Jesus Christ, and love one another, as he gave us commandment.

"And he that keepeth his commandments dwelleth in him, and he in him. And hereby we know that he abideth in us, by the Spirit which he hath given us."

This is now our designation of God, that we also shall be *minded* as was Jesus Christ on earth (Philippians 2). That is our *first change* to His image, according to the Spirit or inner man and our outer life, so that when we are revealed, we shall be *like Him* and known of Him as His own. For at His return, the children of God still await only their *second change* to His image, according to the body, for the complete presentation of conformability to Him, for as we now bear the image of His humiliation and of His holy life, thus shall we then also bear the image of His exhaltation and glorification (Philippians 2; I Corinthians 15).

According to the spirit, we shall not be different in the future world from what we have been or have become here, but shall receive according to what we have done during the life of the body, be it good or evil (II Corinthians 5). That is why we should make it our business (as a matter of honor) as long as we are in the body (in a foreign country and strange land), to please God well and to be without blame before Him (Ephesians 1:4; II Peter 3:14):

> "According as he hath chosen us in him before the foundation of the world, that we should be holy and without blame before him in love:"

> ———

> "Wherefore, beloved, seeing that ye look for such things, be diligent that ye may be found of him in peace, without spot, and blameless."

because only when our heart does not condemn ('withstand' in Galatians 2:11) us, do we have joyousness toward God in the Spirit, with the confidence that from Him we receive what we ask for and have need of, so that we trust not in men or take flesh for our arm, like carnal men, who are accursed on that account (Jeremiah 17).

But because this freeness toward God is based upon

our keeping His commandments — consequently upon our obedience, we shall know that John means, not the commandments of the old law which forbid only the evil, but the new, positive law of the Spirit which imposes upon us the practice of everything that is good in the *one* commandment of love, which comprises all in itself and which is already transgressed by the omission of doing the good, even though one should not do the opposite (evil). *In the New Testament, he who does not do the good sins just as much as one in the Old Testament who does the evil* (James 4: 17).

> "Therefore to him that knoweth to do good, and doeth it not, to him it is sin."

Indeed John mentions two commandments: faith in Christ and love to the brethren. However both are fundamentally one and differ only in prospect. We must cling to Christ by faith so that we are able to *love* and to repay to the brethren what the Lord has done for us. Faith is the *root*, love is the *fruit* and when John puts the two expressions side by side: "Keep his commandments, and do those things that are pleasing in his sight," that is not entirely the same either, but the latter is still higher and greater than the first, for *by keeping His commandments,* we do only our bounden duty and, in spite of it, would still be *unprofitable* servants because we must do it (Luke 17: 10),

> "So likewise ye, when ye shall have done all those things which are commanded you, say, We are unprofitable servants: we have done that which was our duty to do."

would to a certain degree be of the law again. But God the Lord wishes for spontaneous, perfect children who serve Him with pleasure and not merely because they must. Therefore, as love is in relation to the brethren and faith is in relation to Christ, *so the doing of those things that are pleasing to God is in relation to the Father and that extends itself much farther still and no express commandment is given to us for what we every moment have to do so as to be acceptable to the Father. Only the indwelling law of the Spirit of Christ teaches us that.*

Chapter XCI

Asking and Receiving

May 11, 1841 (Tuesday) ; Evening Meeting
I John 3 : 21 f.

> "Beloved, if our heart condemn us not, then have we confidence toward God.
> "And whatsoever we ask, we receive of him, because we keep his commandments, and do those things that are pleasing in his sight."

Since John says: "And whatsoever we ask, we receive of him," the question is whether or not this is to be understood unconditionally and without exception, that we may ask the Father for all that we desire; i.e., what we lack and what is necessary, or about what weighs upon our heart? Yes, by all means; for a purchased child of God will not ask for anything evil and for the good we may and shall ask, of which we know that it is in accordance with the will of God, so that we ask not in vain (chapter 5 : 14 f.) :

> "And this is the confidence that we have in him, that, if we ask any thing according to his will, he heareth us:

> "And if we know that he hear us, whatso-
> ever we ask, we know that we have the peti-
> tions that we desired of him."

and indeed not only for the spiritual, but also for the material things that are needful for us (Matthew 6).

However for asking and receiving, it is necessary that our heart be *pure* and our conscience clear before God and that we sincerely forgive our debtors as God has forgiven us in Christ, not only of all our guilt of the time of ignorance, but still daily forgives us our debts if we confess them and ask for pardon, for if we fail to forgive the faults and debts of others against us, we lose our own pardoning before God (Matthew 5: 23 f.; 18: 21 ff.), and our conduct toward men therefore is the measure by which God deals with us.

> "Therefore if thou bring thy gift to the altar, and there rememberest that thy brother hath ought against thee;
> "Leave there thy gift before the altar, and go thy way; first be reconciled to thy brother, and then come and offer thy gift."

> "Then came Peter to him, and said, Lord, how oft shall my brother sin against me, and I forgive him? till seven times?
> "Jesus saith unto him, I say not unto thee, Until seven times: but, Until seventy times seven.
> "Therefore is the kingdom of heaven likened unto a certain king, which would take account of his servants.
> "And when he had begun to reckon, one was brought unto him, which owed him ten thousand talents.

"But forasmuch as he had not to pay, his lord commanded him to be sold, and his wife, and children, and all that he had, and payment to be made.

"The servant therefore fell down, and worshipped him, saying, Lord, have patience with me, and I will pay thee all.

"Then the lord of that servant was moved with compassion, and loosed him, and forgave him the debt.

"But the same servant went out, and found one of his fellowservants, which owed him an hundred pence: and he laid hands on him, and took him by the throat, saying, Pay me that thou owest.

"And his fellowservant fell down at his feet, and besought him, saying, Have patience with me, and I will pay thee all.

"And he would not: but went and cast him into prison, till he should pay the debt.

"So when his fellowservants saw what was done, they were very sorry, and came and told unto their lord all that was done.

"Then his lord, after that he had called him, said unto him, O thou wicked servant, I forgave thee all that debt, because thou desiredst me:

"Shouldest not thou also have had compassion on thy fellowservant, even as I had pity on thee?

"And his lord was wroth, and delivered him to the tormentors, till he should pay all that was due unto him.

"So likewise shall my heavenly Father do also unto you, if ye from your hearts forgive not every one his brother their trespasses."

Further, we shall ask in faith and not doubt that we shall receive our petition as certainly as we make it known to God (Philippians 4; James 1) for God is honored by our expecting it of Him and receiving it from Him; and even when we are not entirely sure about something—whether we shall really receive our petition or not—and the wisdom of God would have to refuse us for our good, as we see this of Jesus Himself (Matthew 26) and of Paul (II Corinthians 12), still, in simplicity and faith, we shall ask confidently, upon the condition however that the Father finds it a good thing to grant. A refusal is an answer as well as the granting, and *that* we must leave to God Who knows better what is good and wholesome for us than we know it. Conclusively, there should be a real earnestness in our asking, that we may not say something with our lips that our heart knows nothing of, as is generally the case with the Lord's Prayer (*Vater Unser*) by name, which is sinned most against, because if for appearance's sake one inquires of the Lord and wishes to ask something of Him and still has purposed in his heart to have *his own will* and to walk in his own ways, without regard for God's Word and way, it then is an abomination before God (Jeremiah 42; Ezekiel 14 and 20 and 33 : 30 ff.).

"Also, thou son of man, the children of thy people still are talking against thee by the walls and in the doors of the houses, and speak one to another, every one to his brother, saying, Come, I pray you, and hear what is the word that cometh forth from the Lord.

"And they come unto thee as the people cometh, and they sit before thee as my people, and they hear thy words, but they will not do them: for with their mouth they shew much

405

love, but their heart goeth after their covetousness.

"And, lo, thou art unto them as a very lovely song of one that hath a pleasant voice, and can play well on an instrument: for they hear thy words, but they do them not.

"And when this cometh to pass, (lo, it will come,) then shall they know that a prophet hath been among them."

To be sure, the Lord Jesus has given us advice about what we should ask of the Father or what the concern of our heart should be so that we may *surely be heard* if we are in earnest. We should take care that we have and suffer no other will in our heart while we pray the Father: "Thy will be done in earth, as it is in heaven," but should in full confidence pray for it that the Lord may hear us, and then if that which *is* the will of God and what His wisdom considers good comes to pass, we shall not resist His guidance, even though it would perhaps not be according to *our* will or to our limited wisdom and knowledge, but in all that happens to us, we should humble ourselves under the mighty hand of God and cast all our cares upon Him so that, in due time, He may exalt us, in the full assurance that *that* is the will of God and the favorable granting of our petition! Should we then complain when we receive what we have prayed for? Should we not rather rejoice? For if we ourselves know better we need not call upon God.

May 14, 1841 (Friday) ; Evening Meeting
I John 3 : 21

The promise that lies in these words, *"And whatsoever we ask, we receive of him,"* is a great one. But like all promises of God, this one is not unconditional to all men either, but conditional upon our obedience to God, "because we keep his commandments and do those things that are pleasing in his sight." To explain: All promises of God are only in Christ *Yea and Amen,* and not *out* of Christ; they are given and affirmed only to those who, through the one Mediator Jesus, have entered into the covenant of God and stand in fellowship with God the Father as His children, for the covenant of grace is not one-sided but reciprocal, and even though on the part of God it consists of promise after promise and blessing after blessing and man on his part can bring *nothing* except a willing heart, yet afterwards he must apply and use the grace and gift received from Christ and fulfil the obligations and conditions under which alone the promises he has from God are fulfilled (John 14: 21 ff.; 13 f.; II Peter 1: 3 f.).

> "He that hath my commandments, and keepeth them, he it is that loveth me: and he that loveth me shall be loved of my Father, and I will love him, and will manifest myself to him.
> "Judas saith unto him, not Iscariot, Lord, how is it that thou wilt manifest thyself unto us, and not unto the world?
> "Jesus answered and said unto him, If a man love me, he will keep my words: and my Father will love him, and we will come unto him, and make our abode with him.
> "He that loveth me not keepeth not my sayings: and the word which ye hear is not mine, but the Father's which sent me."

> "And whatsoever ye shall ask in my name, that will I do, that the Father may be glorified in the Son.

"If ye shall ask any thing in my name, I will do it.

"If ye love me, keep my commandments."

"According as his divine power hath given unto us all things that pertain unto life and godliness, through the knowledge of him that hath called us to glory and virtue:

"Whereby are given unto us exceeding great and precious promises: that by these ye might be partakers of the divine nature, having escaped the corruption that is in the world through lust."

But that an untrue, untoward, embittered heart is unupright before God and has no part or inheritance in the Word or the promise, we see by Simon the sorcerer (Acts 8), and by the whole world, where all wish to comfort themselves with God's promises but still do not *have* them because they do not fulfil the conditions, for where are there people who have such joyousness [confidence] in God that they ask and then receive from Him what they have asked for?

Most people do not even *ask* or in their distress call upon the living God, Whom they do not know, but take their refuge in vain things. God is never the First with them but always the Last. Others ask and notwithstanding receive nothing because they ask amiss (James 4). Certainly, God keeps His covenant and does not lie in His promises, but just from this it is clear that men *on their part* do not keep the covenant: indeed have never even entered into it and have never obtained the promises of God—forgiveness of sin and the gift of the Holy Spirit and the favorable hearing of their prayers and everlasting salvation—for into the covenant of God no one can enter without knowledge through *conviction,* and consent, which is not the case in infant baptism or in confirmation.

With the rest of the promises of God, it is true, one can more easily comfort oneself falsely, but with asking and receiving [prayer and answer to prayer], there can be no mistake about whether one is in Christ or not, i.e., in the covenant of God, and where this is not the case, there the rest is not to be found either. For, from beginning to end, one thing is dependent upon another and especially is a holy life the condition of answerable prayer. Nor will any excuse avail, as if the requirements were too difficult, for the ability to fulfil them is not of us but is God's gift.

Therefore, he who does not live godly in Christ does not keep the commandments of God, has neither the gift of the Holy Spirit nor the forgiveness of his former sins, can neither pray to be heard nor to be saved. For Christ, the Mediator of the New Testament, is as near to us as to His Father because He is both the Son of God and the Son of man and through Him we shall become so closely related to God that we can call upon Him as our Father, in the confidence that He hears us and grants our prayer, for should He Who has made the *eye* and the *ear* not see and hear? And just this is the right knowledge of God, that we know Him as an all-pervading Spirit.

May 16, 1841 (Sunday) ; Morning Meeting
I John 3 : 21 ff.

"Beloved, if our heart condemn us not, then have we confidence toward God.

"And whatsoever we ask, we receive of him, because we keep his commandments, and do those things that are pleasing in his sight.

> "And this is his commandment, That we
> should believe on the name of his Son Jesus
> Christ, and love one another, as he gave us
> commandment.

> "And he that keepeth his commandments
> dwelleth in him, and he in him. And hereby
> we know that he abideth in us, by the Spirit
> which he hath given us."

Keeping of the commandments of God is the most important thing for a Christian because upon it depends his confidence toward God and the granting of his prayers. But John mentions only two commandments which we have to keep, faith in Christ and love to the brethren. However in faith love is included as in a box. Indeed Peter puts eight such boxes into one another (II Peter I: 5 ff.).

> "And besides this, giving all diligence, add
> to your faith virtue; and to virtue knowledge;

> "And to knowledge temperance; and to
> temperance patience; and to patience godli-
> liness;

> "And to godliness brotherly kindness; and
> to brotherly kindness charity."

To our faith we shall add power (virtue, ability), to power knowledge (understanding, wisdom, prudence) and to knowledge temperance (mastery of self), to temperance patience (endurance), to patience godliness, to godliness brotherly love and to brotherly love the love of our neighbor, charity, so that faith is the first, love however the last (innermost and highest) demonstration of one and the same Spirit—so that we may never think faith is such an easy, empty, ordinary, uninteresting thing as those of the world think, that all are believers, whereas the true faith of Christ is a rare, a difficult, an unusual thing since not all men have faith (II Thessalonians 3:2). Certainly the slothful, false faith of worldly people meets with no difficulty or contradiction for it is of the devil and his great power for hurling the deceived into everlasting destruction.

But the true faith for salvation leads only through combat and suffering, from beginning to end. All rise up against it and resist with all their might—the devil and the world, the members of one's family and one's friends; yes, even one's own unbelief of heart most of all—until one has forced one's way through, for in faith Christ is both hidden and revealed, from His first embryonic stage in which He is sown as the Word, onward until His perfection and development to the stature of manhood in the Spirit, whereunto all believers must attain (Ephesians 4), so that the entire remainder of our life is a life in the faith of the Son of God (Galatians 2) and hid with Him in God (Colossians 3).

But Christ first enters in man as the seed of the new birth and the new life from God (Matthew 13). The word of the preaching of the Crucified Christ as the One Who has died for our sins, for the believing one is the embryo of eternal life. This Word from the Cross falls into the heart of the poor sinner and must molder away in him in order that it may spring up, grow, and bring forth fruit in patience, to its full form and uniformity to the life of Christ on earth (Romans 10). *Faith comes by hearing (preaching), but preaching from the Word of God.*

Afterwards—if one has died with Christ—faith (the kingdom of God within) in a threefold development proceeds onward to its perfection: the first is the shooting grass or childhood, then it is still winter; the second is the standing stalk with the ear or young manhood, then it is spring; the third is the full, ripe fruit in the ear or manhood (fathers in Christ) and then it is summer. But of all who hear the Word (of the world it is not even a question here), scarcely the fourth part attain the goal of salvation. Some right from the beginning do not receive the Word: the devil snatches it away from them so that they by no means believe or are saved (Luke 8). Others die already in childhood by falling away in persecution. The third part attain the age of young manhood but are choked by thorns and it does not come to the fruit or to the end of faith. Therefore Paul says (Hebrews 10): "Ye have need of patience, ... but if any draw back, my soul shall have no pleasure in him." (See also James 1.)

Chapter XCII

"From Faith to Faith"

May 16, 1841 (Sunday) ; Afternoon Meeting
(a continuation)

We might think it a strange commandment that is committed to us from God in the New Testament, that we shall simply believe on the name of Jesus Christ His Son, and yet in this one commandment "all"—the whole life of the Christian — lies, from the beginning of his career unto the end (II Corinthians 5: 7).

"(For we walk by faith, not by sight:)"

For faith has a beginning, a progression and an end (I Peter 1: 9; Hebrews 3: 14)

> "Receiving the end of your faith, even the salvation of your souls."

> "For we are made partakers of Christ, if we hold the beginning of our confidence stedfast unto the end."

and Christ is Himself the Alpha and Omega, the Author and Finisher of Faith (Hebrews 12), and the perfected fighter Paul at the end of his life knew of nothing higher to say of himself than this, "I have kept the faith (II Timothy 4)." But the faith of the beginning, in its course is another than the faith of perfection, for in Christ it goes onward from faith to faith (Romans 1:16)

> "For I am not ashamed of the gospel of Christ: for it is the power of God unto salvation to every one that believeth; to the Jew first, and also to the Greek."

and as Paul, for beginners, would know nothing save Jesus Christ *the Crucified* so as to lay the foundation with the Word from the Cross, which however is a stumbling block to the Jews and foolishness to the Greeks (the self-wise), but to them that are called a power and the wisdom of God unto salvation, so he would know nothing else for the chosen of God than Jesus Christ the *Risen,* the *Living One,* Who sits at the right of God and by the Spirit of Promise would glorify *Himself* in us by His holy life (John 16 and 17).

In the *beginning,* faith has, namely, the cross-character of justification for the past life of sin, but *afterwards* it takes on the cross-character of its work, of suffering and of overcoming unto sanctification and salvation, that nothing at all is any longer able to separate us from Christ (I Corinthians 1 and 2; Galatians 5 and 6). For he who has once been justified by faith in the blood of Christ must afterwards *by faith* live in the Spirit of Christ and just by that *life* be justified in the end before the judgment seat of Christ (Romans I: 17; 5: 21),

> "For therein is the righteousness of God revealed from faith to faith: as it is written, The just shall live by faith."

> "That as sin hath reigned unto death, even so might grace reign through righteousness unto eternal life by Jesus Christ our Lord."

as evidence that he has put on Christ in baptism, which follows upon faith (Galatians 3: 26).

> "For ye are all the children of God by faith in Christ Jesus."

It, however, is always faith by which man must become justified before God. In the beginning it is faith for the forgiveness and cleansing of the former sins and afterwards, the working and overcoming faith, for as the former attaches itself to the Crucified Christ and endures but for a moment, so the latter holds itself to Christ Who sits at the right of God and must remain and be effectual the rest of one's life. That is why "By faith" is mentioned so often in the eleventh chapter of the Epistle to the Hebrews, when the saints of old had received evidence, wrought righteousness, etc., and there is nothing so needful for all children of God as to be reminded ever and again of the old commandment of faith, so that they do not become weary in working and suffering for Christ, in order to do that which is pleasing in the sight of God. And as hard and as important as the beginning of faith is in order to lay the right foundation, so hard and important also is the following faith of obedience in order that the house of God, namely Christ in us the hope of glory, may be built upon this foundation.

In reference to the first faith, Jesus told the Jews who asked Him: "What shall we do that we might work the works of God?", "This is the work of God, that ye believe on him whom he hath sent (John 6)." And afterwards this faith of the Son of God ever continues onward and all who are actually saved, are saved by this: that they abide in faith and work righteousness and overcome the world. It depends upon the right foundation having been laid in the beginning, by faith in the Crucified Christ; not as the world makes Him as One Who ministers to sin and thereupon carelessly continues in sin, counting upon the blood of Christ and the grace of God. And when one inquires about the fruit of faith, about the power of godliness, about the mastery of self, about charity, etc., he finds the opposite of these in them all because they have never truly believed on Christ but only think they believe. Where the foundation has not been laid rightly, there the doing of the will of God does not follow and the house will not remain standing (Matthew 7). Only he who has rightly understood the death of Christ for sin as a *poor* sinner can afterwards overcome with Christ.

Chapter XCIII

Pray and Work

May 18, 1841 (Tuesday); Evening Meeting
I John 3 : 21 ff.

John puts two things in close connection to each other: praying and working, and the one depends upon and sustains the other. Both must go hand in hand. (Even a proverb says "Pray and work!") If our prayer is to be acceptable to God, it is necessary for us to keep His commandments (practise obedience) and, again, if we at all times are to do what is pleasing in the sight of God we must pray without ceasing, in the Spirit cleave to Christ and abide in Him, for without Him we can do nothing that is good. We ourselves do not, independently, have the self-sustaining fountain in us but it is in Christ, and of His fulness we shall take grace for grace; we must receive from above what we shall here below again give and pour forth to the glorification of God. Christ Himself must be in us and, through us, work *all* the will of the Father and if He dwells in us and we abide in Him, certainly the water of life He gives us will be a fountain in us again that flows into eternal life.

By nature dead in sin and the disposition of the flesh, in Adam dead trees, we by no means can do the acceptable will of God, for no one can give *himself* the power of life lost in Adam (Romans 8 : 5 ff.).

> "For they that are after the flesh do mind the things of the flesh; but they that are after the Spirit the things of the Spirit.
> "For to be carnally minded is death; but to be spiritually minded is life and peace.

> "Because the carnal mind is enmity against
> God: for it is not subject to the law of God,
> neither indeed can be.
> "So then they that are in the flesh cannot
> please God."

But if we of ourselves are weak, incapable, and enemies
of God (Romans 3:10 f.; 5:6 ff.), how then shall we
keep the commandments of God and do what is pleasing
in His sight?

> "As it is written, There is none righteous,
> no, not one:
> "There is none that understandeth, there
> is none that seeketh after God."

> "For when we were yet without strength,
> in due time Christ died for the ungodly.
> "For scarcely for a righteous man will one
> die: yet peradventure for a good man some
> would even dare to die.
> "But God commendeth his love toward us,
> in that, while we were yet sinners, Christ died
> for us."

The unraveling of this knot and seeming contradiction
lies in Christ and in our faith on His name. There, the
imagined strength of the one and the weakness with
which the other would excuse himself for not being able
to do the will of God, both disappear. For in Christ the
power that is lost in Adam resides, and if we by faith and
baptism have been planted with Him and by engrafting
into Him have become participants of His sap and stam-
ina, we are enabled to do all things through Him, Who
makes us powerful and efficient, capable of doing all the
good, acceptable and perfect will of God.

It is therefore not man himself but it is Christ the Son

of God Who still, even now, comes (in the flesh) as the Promised Holy Spirit of Power and Love and works all the good in the children of God; dwells in them and walks among them on earth and glorifies the Father so that the rest of the people also, *in the saints,* shall see and learn to know the Father and the Son, just as in the unbelievers the devil works all the evil. Man therefore always serves one master and is a vessel and tool either of honor or dishonor—of grace or of wrath—and no one can serve as a tool for both lords, the devil and Christ, at the same time, but he who does the good, does not do the evil and he who serves the devil, does not serve Christ.

This great change in man comes about by rebirth and the renewal through the Holy Spirit, that he who has hitherto wrought wickedness in obedience to the devil, now works righteousness in obedience to God, and then we shall see to it that we do not again lose the grace of God so that we do not twice become dead trees. We shall so let Christ dwell and live in us that His divine power may continually flow on through us, in order that we live and work in His name on earth to the honor of God the Father; for he who would do the good of his own strength, as well as he who would take refuge in his natural weakness for the good, denies Christ the Son of God in the deed, as if He had not come to destroy the works of the devil by His death or to establish the working of God in us by His eternal life.

For the same Christ Who 1800 years ago personally appeared in the flesh so as to do all the will of the Father, ever appears again through the personality of His Spirit, to perform His redemption work in all who receive Him, and in them and through them does all that is pleasing in the sight of God. Then it is so far removed that we could excuse ourselves with *our own weakness,* that we should rather glory in our weakness, so that the power of Christ may fill us and be the glory in us and we the same in Him. In this way we may boast of Him.

May 20, 1841 (Ascension Thursday) ; Morning Meeting
I John 3 : 22 ff.

"And whatsoever we ask, we receive of him, because we keep his commandments, and do those things that are pleasing in his sight.

"And this is his commandment, That we should believe on the name of his Son Jesus Christ, and love one another, as he gave us commandment.

"And he that keepeth his commandments dwelleth in him, and he in him. And hereby we know that he abideth in us, by the Spirit which he hath given us."

The Christian's spirit is in a continuous two-way movement, upward toward Christ, the Head of the body, the church, and downward toward the brethren as fellow members. What we receive from above through the prayer of faith, we shall *again* out of love give here below. Freely we have received it and freely we shall give it. By faith in Christ, we receive and keep the Holy Spirit, Christ's Representative, the pledge of the inheritance, and the law of the life in Christ which makes us free from the law of sin and death (Romans 8) and which awakens a homesickness in us for that which is above, where Christ now sits at the right hand of God (Colossians 3). And precisely this is why our life is a life in the faith of the Son of God: because He has been removed from our vision, and as one who has departed this life on earth has nothing more to seek or to lose, so it is also with us if we have died and risen with Christ and are placed at the right of God in heaven.

It is a twofold, reciprocal penetration—Christ in us and we in Christ; two in One (Ephesians 5) as in matrimony: our spirit, our longing and sighing is with Him and goes to Him and His Spirit is with us. It is like a mutual longing of love between Christ and His church for the revelation of glory (Romans 8), for now we are still in the proving school where we must endure with Christ in His temptations, in a position of lowliness (Luke 22:28; Philippians 2)

> "Ye are they which have continued with
> me in my temptations."

and Christ longs still more for His revelation than we long for it, so that His heart is inflamed in love toward us, as was Joseph's for his brethren, although he met them with harshness to determine whether they would deal as treacherously with his brother Benjamin as they had previously dealt with him, himself.

But Christ cannot reveal Himself until the time of the Father is fulfilled. He must still *disguise* Himself: speaks through an Interpreter (the Holy Spirit) and presents Himself as stern to put our faith and sincerity to the test, whether or not we will do better with the renewed Image of God (Christ in us) than Adam did with Joseph, whom he sold into bondage; and it is this same bartered Joseph Who stands before us now in another form, as the Exalted One at the right hand of the Father and the Glorified Lord of Glory, and we are not aware that it is Christ Who tries us so severely.

But He cannot do otherwise, as much as it pains Him, for it must be proved to the devil that we love Christ (the renewed image of God in us) more than our own life in this world, and if Adam fell on account of wilfulness and lusting and forfeited the image of God, we must now remain stedfast in all suffering and in every affliction and temptation, and not sell Christ anew. That is why we are given over to the outward power of the devil and the world and are accounted as sheep for the slaughter—considered as fools, persecuted, hated and suppressed—if we are in earnest about godliness, and with all the injustice and unrighteousness we are not permitted to open our mouth, with but a look to Christ Who first suffered for us and now still suffers in us so that we also may be glorified with Him.

For man does not know the true Christ and living Spirit, that He wishes to dwell and walk in us so as again to set up in us the lost kingdom and image of God, against the day of redemption and the revelation of the children of God, for he who does not have in him the pledge of the Spirit of Christ is not His and cannot inherit with Him and be saved. Now, if we would say that Adam did miserably, then, instead of doing likewise, we should do better if, by the power of God, we have been converted, saved and restored from the fall in Adam and have recognized and bewailed our former servitude of sin.

Chapter XCIV

Faith Is the Entrance Door to Christ

May 20, 1841 (Ascension Thursday) ;
Afternoon Meeting (a continuation)

John, so trustingly and confidently, says in his and his brothers' name, "We keep his commandments, and do those things that are pleasing in his sight." Has he not said too much concerning this and has he not been deceived? But since he has told the pure truth, we should take care that it may be true of us also, for if they could do it, we should also be able to, provided we now follow them in the same simple faith on the name of Christ the Son (John 1:12; II Peter 1:1).

> "But as many as received him, to them gave he power to become the sons of God, even to them that believe on his name:"

> "Simon Peter, a servant and an apostle of Jesus Christ, to them that have obtained like precious faith with us through the righteousness of God and our Saviour Jesus Christ:"

Then if we ask "How can we attain to this so as to enter into Christ, put Him on, and of Him and in Him become partakers of all the strength that is needed for life and godliness?" the answer is "Believe on the name of the Lord Jesus."

Faith is the door of entry to Christ and this door is open to all if they are but meek. But just this is what is lacking, for men seek many artifices and because of their craftiness never attain to the power of godliness but testify of a false faith and an appearance of godliness. To explain, if one does not enter in and pass over by the first faith of justification and, accordingly, does not go out from sin and the fellowship of the devil, Christ cannot enter into him through the Holy Spirit of Promise in order to establish again the image of God in him (which is Christ Himself and only Christ); for this new creation in man is merely the seal of faith—a setting of the seal to it—that man *by the faith of the truth* has entered into Christ, no longer to live to himself but to the Lord Who died and arose for us; indeed that Christ might live in us for God and do all the good, acceptable and perfect will of the Father, as it is written (Ephesians 2; II Corinthians 5):

> "For we are his workmanship, created in Christ Jesus unto good works, ..."

> "Therefore if any man be in Christ, he is a new creature: old things are passed away; behold, all things are become new."

But if all things are new, then all things have become good, as it was in the beginning (Genesis 1), for the new work of God is not, in addition, an evil one but an entirely *good* one because it is the image of God (Christ the Son) Who dwells and lives in man and no longer the man himself or the devil in him (Galatians 2). Then all things are not only new and good in *each one* but all are *new* and *one* who have entered into Christ and Christ has entered into them. Here, there is no longer Greek, Jew, Barbarian, Reformed, Catholic, etc., but *all* and *in all* Christ and all are but one only in Him (Galatians 3; Colossians 3), a fellowship of saints indeed, or Christ's body, for He Himself, the Head, is in heaven and invisible until His revelation in glory and, with Him, all that are His. Thus the believers are not only one among themselves but one with Him also, one body and one Spirit (Ephesians 4), and one knows and distinguishes true believers from false ones by nothing else than the life of Christ or the image of God which is revealed in them unto the Day of Redemption, and by His Spirit Christ comes into our flesh to glorify the Father on earth in His saints so that the rest of the people may learn to know God also and in Christ find the way to the Father, i.e., to eternal life. In all who are born of God (children of God), one should recognize the image of God because Christ the Son is in them. Paul therefore says (II Corinthians 13:5):

> "Examine yourselves, whether ye be in the faith; prove your own selves. Know ye not your own selves, how that Jesus Christ is in you, except ye be reprobates?"

All, therefore, depends upon faith, for he who abides in faith abides in Christ. But *in him* who abides in Christ, Christ most certainly also abides and by this, by the Spirit He has given us as the seal of the righteousness of faith and the pledge of the inheritance, we know that He abides in us, for all children of God are also predestined heirs of God and joint heirs with Christ, i.e., provided they abide in faith and hold fast the beginning of their confidence to the end (Hebrews 3). Christ in us as the hope of glory is the only evidence and proof we have that we are in Christ and whoever does not have Christ's Spirit of life is not His because he does not believe on Him, and this is his own fault.

That is why God has made the way to life and redemption so easy for us, so that the meek could be saved, and the rest will be lost on their own account. Had God demanded great and difficult things of us, we might perhaps be able to excuse ourselves, but since all that He asks of us is faith on the name of the Son Jesus Christ, no unbeliever has any excuse for he is disobedient to the command of God, "Believe and thou shalt be saved!" For the sealing of this faith however, man must be baptized so as actually to put Christ on and receive the affirmation of justification in the Holy Spirit.

Therefore, the first requirement for a holy life in Christ in the power of godliness is that we be in Christ and Christ be in us; and the second, that we abide in Him and

He abide in us, for what proved effectual with the apostles on a large scale, "Except ye abide in me, ye can do nothing," proves to be so also with each believer on a small scale and in particular (John 15:4).

("Abide in me, and I in you. As the branch cannot bear fruit of itself, except it abide in the vine; no more can ye, except ye abide in me.")

But for entering in in Christ, nothing more is required than a thorough conversation from the power of Satan to God and calling upon the Lord, for as soon as one himself decides for Christ, so soon also must Satan release him, since Christ came for this, that He might free and release the captives and prisoners from the devil when they hear His voice and will no longer remain willingly in Satan's power (Luke 4).

We shall, therefore, be assured that there is a state of grace in which men of God do the will of the Father and sin no more, because sin is the opposite of the good pleasure of God (for the carnally minded cannot please Him, Romans 8), and because Christ (in us) according to His nature cannot sin but at all times does that which is pleasing to God. However if Christ is not in us, we are not in Him either, i.e., we are unbelieving and unqualified for eternal blessedness.

But because we renounce the devil and enter into opposition and disagreement with the whole world as soon as we are converted to Christ and have His life in us, we have the devil and the whole world as enemies, who, in all directions, obstruct the way of life for us and would like again to turn us from it and, then, only the firm faith in Christ is able to overcome, and where our faith does not have a world-overcoming power, it cannot endure unto the end along with Christ in the good fight that is set before us in the world (Philippians 2). Therefore we need only to cleave firmly to our Head, Christ, Who at the right hand of God is lifted up above all things.

Chapter XCV

Stedfast Faith

May 23, 1841 (Sunday) ; Morning Meeting
I John 3 : 22 ff.

What John says here of an abiding faith and of a dwelling in Christ does not hold good for the people of the world (who are not in Christ), but only for the children of God and has the intention that these who by faith and baptism have been restored from Adam's fall and *stand* in Christ, shall *continue* to stand and shall not again fall from grace and the truth (I Corinthians 10), which is indeed possible since the devil walks about and seeks whomever he may devour. We must now firmly resist him in faith and not take offense at the tribulation, knowing that these sufferings befall and have befallen the entire brotherhood of Christ in this world (I Peter 5), and that only those can fall who actually stand.

But *in Adam* all have fallen and no one stands. Therefore rising from Adam's death and fall is the first condition and requirement. In what does Adam's fall consist? In the divestiture of the image of God (the righteousness and holiness of the truth), into the place of which the image of the devil has entered (death and sin). But because Christ as the Lamb of God died and arose for this, to bear and to reconcile the sin of all the world, and, by His death and resurrection, has presented *all men righteous* (just as by Adam's fall all men have become sinners), God, for Christ's sake, no longer imputes to them their sins of the time of ignorance. For as we without our cooperation have become sinners, so are we also without our cooperation reconciled (Romans 5; II Corinthians 5). Now each one who hears the Gospel must choose for himself life or death; and as the believer is saved and reestablished in Christ, so the unbeliever, on account of his own guilt (not Adam's), falls a prey to eternal death (John 3:16 ff.; 16:8 ff.),

"For God so loved the world, that he gave his only begotten Son, that whosoever believeth in him should not perish, but have everlasting life.

"For God sent not his Son into the world to condemn the world; but that the world through him might be saved.

"He that believeth on him is not condemned: but he that believeth not is condemned already, because he hath not believed in the name of the only begotten Son of God.

"And this is the condemnation, that light is come into the world, and men loved darkness rather than light, because their deeds were evil.

"For every one that doeth evil hateth the light, neither cometh to the light, lest his deeds should be reproved.

"But he that doeth truth cometh to the light, that his deeds may be made manifest, that they are wrought in God.

> "And when he is come, he will reprove the world of sin, and of righteousness, and of judgment:
>
> "Of sin, because they believe not on me;
>
> "Of righteousness, because I go to my Father, and ye see me no more;
>
> "Of judgment, because the prince of this world is judged."

and in this sense the Holy Ghost says (Luke 2:34) that Christ "is set for the fall and rising again of many in Israel;" (and among all peoples).

The children shall not die on their father Adam's account or be lost through another's guilt, but each one must die for his own sin and guilt, because he does not believe in the word and on name of the Son of God, and according as men *first* by the rejection of salvation fall into eternal death, so believers in Christ rise up from the fall of Adam. This power of rising up lies in the name of Jesus Christ (Acts 4) and through faith on it man is restored, that he might praise God and follow Christ, for those who do not follow Christ have not risen from the death of Adam but only carry on idle talk about faith and their mockery of the Gospel.

Therefore, the nominal Christians are all not only without excuse but they are also responsible, in that they wish to bear the name of Christ and nevertheless serve the devil and do not believe on Christ and then one like the other is dead by nature and unqualified for God— the 'pious' as well as the ungodly. There is only one Door to Salvation for all (Luke 18) and he who does not enter in thereat during the time of grace remains outside in all eternity, for to all is said, "Behold, all things are ready." But some are self-righteous and others love darkness more than light.

But because the pardoned in Christ *can fall again,* as did Adam who was also of the image of God, we must take care that we are not only restored by faith in Christ from Adam's fall and death, but that we also continue to stand in Christ and, without wavering, resist the devil in temptation and walk in the fear of God afterwards, knowing that we have been ransomed at a great price from our vain walk according to the traditions of our fathers, by the blood of Christ (I Peter 1). For the devil fights against the true believers with great might and strategy to encompass them, that they should fall away again by yielding in the life of faith of the Son of God, since our position on earth is one of trial in order that it may be made manifest whether Christ is in us. But if we only abide in Him, we need have no fear that we may be overcome, for Christ is faithful and strong and loves us and willingly abides with us more than we love and abide with Him. If the devil does not hate us, we do not have the true faith in which the living Christ is found and of which the world knows and wishes to know nothing.

Chapter XCVI

The Pilgrim State

May 23, 1841 (Sunday); Afternoon Meeting

"Beloved, if our heart condemn us not, then have we confidence toward God.

"And whatsoever we ask, we receive of him, because we keep his commandments, and do those things that are pleasing in his sight.

"And this is his commandment, That we should believe on the name of his Son Jesus Christ, and love one another, as he gave us commandment.

> "And he that keepeth his commandments dwelleth in him, and he in him. And hereby we know that he abideth in us, by the Spirit which he hath given us."

In these verses (21-24) lies the description of our pilgrim state here on earth in the imitation of Christ: *faith* and *love*. He who believes abides in Christ. But Christ is in heaven at the right of the Father as Lord over All (Hebrews 1 and 2; Ephesians 2), and if we are in Him and continue in Him, then in faith we are also lords and heirs of all things in heaven, in hope (Romans 8), and we let this real exaltedness and *first* glory and His grace be sufficient for us (II Corinthians 3:18; 12:9),

> "But we all, with open face beholding as in a glass the glory of the Lord, are changed into the same image from glory to glory even as by the Spirit of the Lord."

> "And he said unto me, My grace is sufficient for thee: for my strength is made perfect in weakness. Most gladly therefore will I rather glory in my infirmities, that the power of Christ may rest upon me."

without desiring the counterfeit high estate of this world (Romans 12:16).

> "Be of the same mind one toward another. Mind not high things, but condescend to men of low estate. Be not wise in your own conceits."

For arrogance is nothing more than the hereditary disease of all children of Adam, so that all prefer to rule and to be exalted rather than to serve and obey; prefer to sit in a high rather than in a low place, and he who exalts himself shall be abased but he who humbles himself shall be exalted (Luke 18). But Christ, as the Lord, has given us, in Himself, the example of lowliness (washing of feet, John 13; Philippians 2) that we in His footsteps should follow. He was not only lowly and meek at heart but also pure—holy, undefiled, without sin (I Peter 2)—and in both He is our Example.

The *second* glory then follows of itself, since it is understood of itself that we abide in Him if He abides in us. Therefore John mentions only the last token: "And hereby we know that he abideth in us, by the Spirit which he hath given us." But if Christ is in us (i.e., His Spirit, John 16), then His mind and holy life is too, for we cannot think of Christ and not of His mind and life. He cannot deny Himself, and unless He is in one, there can be no Christian; and we know the real Christian not by lofty things and knowledge, etc., but only by love and holiness is it evident that we have received the Spirit of Christ (I Corinthians 12:1 ff.).

> "Now concerning spiritual gifts, brethren, I would not have you ignorant.
>
> "Ye know that ye were Gentiles, carried away unto these dumb idols, even as ye were led.
>
> "Wherefore I give you to understand, that no man speaking by the Spirit of God calleth Jesus accursed: and that no man can say that Jesus is the Lord, but by the Holy Ghost."

However, if Christ is in us, the world hates us, and we must bear His reproach (Romans 15:3);

> "For even Christ pleased not himself; but, as it is written, The reproaches of them that reproached thee fell on me."

—are considered offscourings and an expiatory offering of all men, and we let that please us (II Corinthians 5 and 12). If we but know that, with Christ, we are set as lords over all, then in regard to the earthly we are satisfied with what is here and with the lowliness and servant-form of Christ on earth. For just as we by faith are set in heaven as lords, so are we by love set on earth as servants, willingly however (I Corinthians 9), because Christ in us is not high-minded, strives not after things that are high, but lowers Himself, is obedient unto death, serves, and offers up His life for the brethren. Thus the children of God have a twofold life in Christ: are at the same time exalted and lowly, in heaven and on earth; live in faith and in love, are very glorious inwardly and very inglorious outwardly.

May 25, 1841 (Tuesday); Evening Meeting
I John 3:23 f.

> "And this is his commandment, That we should believe on the name of his Son Jesus Christ, and love one another, as he gave us commandment.

> "And he that keepeth his commandments dwelleth in him and he in him. And hereby we know that he abideth in us, by the Spirit he hath given us."

Faith to Christ, as the commandment of the Father to His children on earth and as a continuous activity, is a full, stedfast, sure confidence toward Christ Who, as the Almighty Lord, sits at the right of God and accordingly reigns over all, so that without His will not even a hair can fall from our head (Matthew 28:18).

> "And Jesus came and spake unto them, saying, All power is given unto me in heaven and in earth."

In this unconditional confidence, our life on earth is entirely as was His life in the days of His flesh (Hebrews 2:13; 5:7 ff.),

> "And again, I will put my trust in him. And again, Behold I and the children which God hath given me."

> "Who in the days of his flesh, when he had offered up prayers and supplications with strong crying and tears unto him that was able to save him from death, and was heard in that he feared;
> "Though he were a Son, yet learned he obedience by the things which he suffered;
> "And being made perfect, he became the author of eternal salvation unto all them that obey him;
> "Called of God an high priest after the order of Melchisedec."

when He lowered, denied, and poured out Himself and became like another man, and, as a servant, was obedient to the Father, submissive to all His will, for Jesus as the Son of man wished to be no higher than any other person so that we as His brethren would have a pattern in Him.

But this faithful confidence toward Christ is twofold: in reference to His guidance of us and in reference to His promise. Both must go hand in hand. For since the Father has given us His Son, we must firmly believe that we are foreordained heirs and lords of all in Him, now already seated in heaven at the right of God, and that all that the Son has is also ours, as if we already actually possessed it so that we may not doubt it in the least.

But if our faith does not bring about unquestioning obedience to His guidance and government, so that in all that may happen to us we may be convinced that it is His will, His Way, His guidance and providence, even if it is displeasing and contrary to our flesh (for God's ways are not our ways just as our thoughts are not His thoughts, and just by this we shall know it is God's way and will, because we would do and choose things otherwise). If we do not humble ourselves under His mighty hand here so that He may exalt us in due time (for now is the time of our abasement and our exaltation then follows of itself if we have learned to be lowly), we deceive ourselves if we hope for the future rest and glory, like all the unconverted who are disobedient to the Gospel and still hope to be saved.

Indeed, if we are not submissive and obedient to all of God's will, we lie when we say that we believe in Christ the Crucified, for if we do not have faith and confidence toward the Christ Who is at the right of God and reigns so as to let ourselves be led according to His counsel that He may eventually receive us into His glory, we cannot believe either that Christ died for our sins. That is why the Israelites of Old are set before us as an example of warning, who indeed by the high hand and outstretched arm of the Lord, with signs and wonders had also gone out of Egypt and yet never believed on Him afterwards, but in each new trial and temptation always murmured again and tempted God, and because of their unbelief (disobedience) could not attain to the promise of rest, for it is always easier to murmur, to be dissatisfied and unruly than to believe, trust, be still, and obedient.

However, by complete faith we honor God, in that we let His wondrous ways please us, for faith of the right sort works patience and patience waits for and obtains the promise of God through a lively hope (Romans 5 and 8). For he who honors God is honored in return by Him. But we honor God in this: that we neither doubt His way nor His promise nor make Him a liar in His Word but endure in all our temptations and trials, for God often tries His own so sorely and severely that to them it seems they are forsaken of God and man. However, faith and confidence that is genuine esteems God faithful and true in His Word and on this dark way attains to the rest of the people of God and to the crown of righteousness and life. Without such obedience and confidence toward God, all faith is merely imagination, an illusion, a deception of the devil.

May 28, 1841 (Friday); Evening Meeting
I John 3:23, 24

> "And this is his commandment, That we should believe on the name of his Son Jesus Christ, and love one another, as he gave us commandment.
>
> "And he that keepeth his commandments dwelleth in him, and he in him. And hereby we know that he abideth in us, by the Spirit which he hath given us."

We should not think it an idle word when John says that Christ must be in us, but should examine ourselves to determine whether Christ's Spirit *is* in us and whether His divine life works in us as the Spirit of Power and Love (II Timothy 1:7).

> "For God hath not given us the spirit of fear; but of power, and of love, and of a sound mind."

For it is just in this way that the true faith and true believer is distinguished from all the false, feigned, dissembling, sham, human behavior (which adorns itself with the name of piety), that Christ *in us* may be a power of God to fulfil all the acceptable will of God, while self-made human piety always remains powerless and even with the best intentions does not bring about the achievement which is however imparted to us by the Spirit of Christ.

In the true, divine faith toward Christ lies a power of overcoming the world and its prince, who, otherwise, still has all men in his power, and where one's faith is united with Christ the Head in Heaven, there love is the bond of perfection that unites all the members among themselves into one. However, where the faith is false, there its love also is false and does not bind together because the spirit of the world forces men to seek their own and not that which is another's and where men are not sanctified by the Spirit, or Christ is not in them, a fellowship of the saints is impossible.

But the Spirit of the Lord is given to all who are rightly converted and born of God. Therefore one cannot represent himself as something that he is not. No false Christian succeeds in living the holy life of Christ, for just as Christ was exalted as the Son of man, so He, as the Son of God, through His Spirit of Truth dwells in all believers and brings about in them:

(a) both a divine enlightenment concerning all the will of God and the confidence and willingness to do it;

(b) both a power of overcoming all things that might

separate them from the love of Christ and a power of offering up themselves for the brethren through the love of Christ (Ephesians 1:15 ff.).

"Wherefore I also, after I heard of your faith in the Lord Jesus, and love unto all the saints,

"Cease not to give thanks for you, making mention of you in my prayers;

"That the God of our Lord Jesus Christ, the Father of glory, may give unto you the spirit of wisdom and revelation in the knowledge of him:

"The eyes of your understanding being enlightened; that ye may know what is the hope of his calling, and what the riches of the glory of his inheritance in the saints,

"And what is the exceeding greatness of his power to us-ward who believe, according to the working of his mighty power,

"Which he wrought in Christ, when he raised him from the dead, and set him at his own right hand in the heavenly places,

"Far above all principality, and power, and might, and dominion, and every name that is named, not only in this world, but also in that which is to come:

"And hath put all things under his feet, and gave him to be the head over all things to the church,

"Which is his body, the fulness of him that filleth all in all."

Therefore, in the knowledge of Christ is found, at the same time, a spirit of wisdom and revelation so that children of God can hold themselves firmly to their invisible Head and may rejoice in the foreglimpse of their eternal life with Christ.

— END OF VOLUME II —